COMPUTER SOLUTION OF

LINEAR ALGEBRAIC SYSTEMS

Aug. 1967

Prentice-Hall

Series in Automatic Computation

George Forsythe, editor

BATES AND DOUGLAS, *Programming Language/One*
BAUMANN, FELICIANO, BAUER, AND SAMELSON, *Introduction to ALGOL*
BOWLES (editor), *Computers in Humanistic Research*
CESCHINO AND KUNTZMAN, *Numerical Solution of Initial Value Problems*
DESMONDE, *Computers and Their Uses*
DESMONDE, *Real-Time Data Processing Systems: Introductory Concepts*
EVANS, WALLACE, AND SUTHERLAND, *Simulation Using Digital Computers*
FORSYTHE AND MOLER, *Computer Solution of Linear Algebraic Systems*
GOLDEN, *FORTRAN IV: Programming and Computing*
HARTMANIS AND STEARNS, *Algebraic Structure Theory of Sequential Machines*
MARTIN, *Programming Real-Time Computer Systems*
MARTIN, *Systems Analysis for Real-Time Computers*
MINSKY, *Computation: Finite and Infinite Machines*
MOORE, *Interval Analysis*
SCHULTZ, *Digital Processing: A System Orientation*
SNYDER, *Chebyshev Methods in Numerical Approximation*
STROUD AND SECREST, *Gaussian Quadrature Formulas*
TRAUB, *Iterative Methods for the Solution of Equations*
VARGA, *Matrix Iterative Analysis*
WILKINSON, *Rounding Errors in Algebraic Processes*

PRENTICE-HALL INTERNATIONAL, INC., *London*
PRENTICE-HALL OF AUSTRALIA, PTY. LTD., *Sydney*
PRENTICE-HALL OF CANADA, LTD., *Toronto*
PRENTICE-HALL OF INDIA PRIVATE LTD., *New Delhi*
PRENTICE-HALL OF JAPAN, INC., *Tokyo*

COMPUTER SOLUTION OF
LINEAR ALGEBRAIC SYSTEMS

GEORGE E. FORSYTHE

Professor of Computer Science
Stanford University

CLEVE B. MOLER

Assistant Professor of Mathematics
University of Michigan

PRENTICE-HALL, INC.

ENGLEWOOD CLIFFS, N.J.

© 1967 by
Prentice-Hall, Inc.
Englewood Cliffs, N.J.

Current printing (last digit):

10 9 8 7 6 5 4 3 2 1

Library of Congress Catalog Card No.: 67-18915

Printed in the United States of America

to James H. Wilkinson

PREFACE

This monograph is intended primarily as a textbook for students of numerical analysis and computer science. It started from teaching a senior-graduate course in numerical analysis at Stanford University with a textbook that devoted almost no attention to matrix problems. Its author advised the reader to expect suitable programs at the computation center and to consult an expert if he got into trouble. In contrast, we believe that students need to understand matrix programs in order to apply them or modify them in unanticipated situations. Moreover, many of our students later write or translate programs for computation centers. To fill the gap, notes were prepared for a unit on matrix computation, and part of those notes has grown into the present monograph. The prerequisites, detailed in Sec. 1, include a course in linear algebra and some knowledge of programming.

In addition to numerical analysts and computer programmers, we feel that students and workers in mathematical programming, statistics, engineering, and the many other fields involving matrices and computation should be familiar with much of this material.

The solution of a system of linear algebraic equations is one of the tasks most frequently encountered in computing. Because linear functions are best understood, the most common models of multivariate functional dependence are linear and lead to linear equation systems. Moreover, most approaches to the solution of nonlinear problems lead to a sequence of linear systems. Because they are so common, it is crucially necessary for a computing laboratory to be able to deal quickly and accurately with linear algebraic systems. It is surprising how often this requirement is not met.

As we state in Sec. 6, linear systems vary widely. One important type is treated above all others in this monograph—the system with a dense, stored matrix of coefficients. The thorough study of one important algorithm for solving it—Gaussian elimination with iterative improvement—forms our central theme. The last sections deal briefly with other methods for solving linear and nonlinear systems.

In comparison with other constructive mathematics, numerical analysis is distinguished by two features:

(1) a concern for such economic issues as running time and storage requirements of algorithms;

(2) an analysis of errors caused by various forms of limited-precision arithmetic in computers.

The first concern makes Gaussian elimination the method of choice for solving dense, stored linear systems. But there are many variants of elimination, and attention to error analysis guides the selection among the alternatives.

In addition to our exposition of Gaussian elimination, with numerical examples and analyses of errors, we present the actual computer algorithm that we consider to be best. To make it widely available, we have given the algorithm in three languages: ALGOL 60, ASA FORTRAN and PL/I. We call explicit attention in Sec. 17 to places where differences in languages or processors make it difficult to translate the program exactly. We believe these programs and the accompanying discussion to be an important contribution of this book.

We dedicate our book to J. H. Wilkinson, who has created so much of numerical analysis. The mature scholar can do no better than study his two books on matrix computations. However, it is not easy for the less advanced student to find his way through the very substantial material in these books. A major portion of the present monograph is devoted to explaining and motivating some of the algorithms and analyses put forward by Wilkinson.

The authors wish to acknowledge the special help of R. W. Hamming, who showed us how little we knew about scaling matrices; J. G. Herriot, who taught from the original notes and criticized them; W. M. McKeeman, who published an early version of the ALGOL 60 program of Sec. 16; B. N. Parlett, who reviewed the entire manuscript; and F. L. Bauer, P. Businger, G. H. Golub, W. Kahan, and J. H. Wilkinson, who suggested improvements in portions of the manuscript. Thanks are also due to the staffs of the computation centers at Stanford University, University of Michigan, Eidgenössische Technische Hochschule, Zurich, and IBM Research Laboratory, Rüschlikon, Switzerland for their help in testing the computer programs. Finally, we acknowledge the partial financial support of the National Science Foundation and the Office of Naval Research.

GEORGE E. FORSYTHE
CLEVE B. MOLER

CONTENTS

I. READER'S BACKGROUND AND PURPOSE OF BOOK

We assume that the reader has had a course in linear algebra, as customarily taught to students of mathematics. We therefore expect him to be familiar with matrices representing linear transformations in given co-ordinate systems and with vectors and their components. We expect that he has been introduced to the basic ideas of equivalence, congruence, and similarity, and to the canonical forms of matrices under these transformations. We presume that he knows the basic facts about determinants and systems of linear equations and about eigenvalues and eigenvectors of matrices. Chapter 1 of Faddeeva (1959) contains a good summary of this material.

We assume that the reader is familiar with programming an automatic digital computer in FORTRAN, ALGOL 60, or PL/I, and that he knows some-thing about numerical computations and their errors but nothing about matrix computations.

The purpose of this book is to bring such a reader as quickly as possible to an understanding of a few good programs for solving linear equation systems and of the fundamental concepts of error involved.

2. VECTOR AND MATRIX NORMS

We assume that the reader is reasonably familiar with the algebra of matrices representing linear transformations. For an understanding of numerical matrix methods one must also be somewhat familiar with the geometry and analysis of matrices as linear transformations, since in computing we are directly concerned with the magnitudes of the different numbers which appear. We give an introduction to these concepts in this section and the next. Again, a more extensive discussion with proofs will be found in Faddeeva (1959), although theorem (3.1) is not in it.

Let $x = (x_1, x_2, \ldots, x_n)^T$ denote a column vector in real n-dimensional space R^n. Let x^T denote the row vector which is the transpose of x. We introduce the concept of the euclidean length or *norm* of a vector x, denoted by $\|x\|$, by defining it as

$$(2.1) \qquad \|x\| = \sqrt{|x_1|^2 + \cdots + |x_n|^2} = \sqrt{x^T x}.$$

The norm has the following properties of ordinary length in two or three dimensions:

$$(2.2) \qquad \|cx\| = |c| \cdot \|x\| \qquad \text{for all real } c \text{ and all vectors } x.$$

$$(2.3) \qquad \|\theta\| = 0 \quad \text{and} \quad \|x\| > 0 \quad \text{if} \quad x \neq \theta.$$

$$\text{(Here } \theta \text{ denotes the null vector.)}$$

$$(2.4) \qquad \|x + y\| \leq \|x\| + \|y\| \qquad \text{for all vectors } x, y.$$

(Equality occurs in (2.4) if and only if x and y are linearly dependent, i.e., are collinear vectors.)

Whereas (2.2) and (2.3) follow directly from (2.1), the proof of (2.4), which is left to the reader, requires elementary analysis. It can be done by first proving the famous Cauchy-Schwarz-Bunyakovskij inequality,

$$(2.5) \qquad |x^T y| \leq \|x\| \cdot \|y\|$$

for any x, y. Inequality (2.5) can be proved by noting that it is a necessary condition for the quadratic function

$$(\alpha x + \beta y)^T (\alpha x + \beta y) = \alpha^2 \|x\|^2 + 2\alpha\beta x^T y + \beta^2 \|y\|^2$$

of the real variables α, β to be nonnegative.

2

We now define the norm of an n-rowed and n-columned real matrix A as

(2.6)
$$\|A\| = \max_{x \neq 0} \frac{\|Ax\|}{\|x\|}.$$

As a direct consequence

(2.7) $\|cA\| = |c| \cdot \|A\|$ for all real c and all A;

(2.8) $\|\Theta\| = 0$ and $\|A\| > 0$ if $A \neq \Theta$

(here Θ denotes the null matrix);

(2.9) $\|A + B\| \leq \|A\| + \|B\|$ for all n-by-n matrices A and B.

These properties are exactly the same as properties (2.2), (2.3), (2.4) for vectors. Thus the set of n-by-n matrices A can be interpreted as a normed vector space of dimension n^2.

It also follows directly from definition (2.6) that

(2.10) $\|Ax\| \leq \|A\| \cdot \|x\|$ for all A, x.

Moreover it follows that inequality (2.10) is always "sharp" or "best possible" —i.e., for each A there exists a vector x so that

(2.11) $\|Ax\| = \|A\| \cdot \|x\|.$

It is left to the reader to prove from (2.6) that

(2.12) $\|AB\| \leq \|A\| \cdot \|B\|$ for all matrices A, B.

It is properties (2.10) and (2.12) which make the vector and matrix norm so very useful in analyzing linear mappings and, in particular, the errors in solving linear systems of equations.

The square matrix A represents a linear transformation (mapping) of each vector x of one n-dimensional space X into the vector $y = Ax$ of a second n-dimensional space Y. Definition (2.6) can be equivalently expressed in the form

(2.13) $\|A\| = \max_{\|x\|=1} \|Ax\|.$

But (2.13) can be interpreted as defining $\|A\|$ to be the length of the longest vector in the image set $\{Ax\}$ of the unit sphere $\{x: \|x\| = 1\}$ under the transformation $x \to Ax$.

Recall that an orthogonal matrix U is characterized by the property $U^T U = U U^T = I$, where I is the unit matrix. The mapping $x \to Ux$ represents a rigid rotation of n space onto itself, possibly preceded by a reflection in some hyperplane.

The euclidean norm (2.1) corresponds to the usual notion of length in two and three dimensions and allows us to use our geometric intuition in higher dimensions. This length is preserved by orthogonal matrices—that is, $\|x\| = \|Ux\|$ for all orthogonal matrices U.

We have actually discussed only one vector norm out of an infinite number which can be defined. Two others which are commonly used in numerical analysis are

$$(2.14) \qquad \qquad \|x\|_1 = \sum_{i=1}^n |x_i|$$

and

$$(2.15) \qquad \qquad \|x\|_\infty = \max_{1 \le i \le n} |x_i|.$$

These vector norms satisfy (2.2), (2.3), (2.4) and, in turn, induce corresponding new matrix norms by an application of (2.6). It is shown, for example, by Faddeeva (1959) that

$$(2.16) \qquad \qquad \|A\|_1 = \max_{1 \le j \le n} \sum_{i=1}^n |a_{i,j}|;$$

$$(2.17) \qquad \qquad \|A\|_\infty = \max_{1 \le i \le n} \sum_{j=1}^n |a_{i,j}|.$$

These two norms do not allow us to use our geometric intuition so freely and their corresponding norm-preserving matrices are not so common as orthogonal matrices. However, the norms (2.16) and (2.17) are easier to compute than the euclidean norm and are quite useful in many applications.

Almost everything we have said in this section can be said also for vectors and matrices of complex numbers. It is only necessary to replace the transpose x^T and A^T by the complex conjugate transpose $x^H = \bar{x}^T$ and $A^H = \bar{A}^T$.

(2.18) **Exercise.** Prove (2.4), (2.12), (2.16), and (2.17).

(2.19) **Exercise.** Show that for any n-by-n matrix A,

$$\max_{i,j} |a_{i,j}| \le \|A\| \le n \max_{i,j} |a_{i,j}|.$$

3. DIAGONAL FORM OF A MATRIX UNDER ORTHOGONAL EQUIVALENCE

We wish to develop some geometric intuition about the nature of a square matrix A as representing a linear transformation of one euclidean n space into another such space. Assume both spaces have given orthogonal coordinate systems. In the authors' opinion the following theorem (3.1) leads to the simplest interpretation of the linear transformation represented by the matrix. Recall that orthogonal matrices were defined in Sec. 2.

(3.1) **Theorem.** *Given any n-by-n real matrix A, there exist two n-by-n real orthogonal matrices U, V so that $U^T A V$ is a diagonal matrix D. Moreover, we may choose U and V so that the diagonal elements of D are*

$$\mu_1 \geq \mu_2 \geq \cdots \geq \mu_r > \mu_{r+1} = \cdots = \mu_n = 0,$$

where r is the rank of A. In particular, if A is nonsingular then

$$\mu_1 \geq \mu_2 \geq \cdots \geq \mu_n > 0.$$

The numbers $\mu_1, \ldots, \mu_n$ are the *singular values* of A. As will be shown later in this section, they are the nonnegative square roots of the (necessarily nonnegative) eigenvalues of the symmetric matrix AA^T, where A^T is the transpose of A. Practically all the important facts for solving a system of equations with the matrix A are linked to the nature of the set of singular values of A. The proof of (3.1) is given in Sec. 4.

Textbooks of linear algebra, when discussing equivalence, customarily state theorem (3.1) with U^T, V replaced by general nonsingular matrices P^{-1}, Q, and with $\mu_1, \ldots, \mu_r$ all replaced by 1. For computational purposes orthogonal matrices U, V are much more valuable because $\|Ux\| = \|x\|$ for any orthogonal matrix U and any vector x. Hence multiplications by orthogonal matrices preserve the magnitudes of the numbers involved, whereas multiplication by a general nonsingular matrix P may alter them drastically. This is an important distinction.

To understand why (3.1) is so useful, consider A as representing a linear transformation of one n-dimensional space X into a second such space Y. Thus $y = Ax$ is in Y for any x in X. In representing the linear transformation by the matrix A we have assumed given orthogonal coordinate systems in both X and Y. Now consider an orthogonal change of coordinates in space

5

X, so that the vector represented above by x obtains the new representation x', where $x = Vx'$. In the same way, by a different orthogonal coordinate change in Y, we obtain a new representation for y, namely y', where $y = Uy'$. Here both U and V are the matrices of (3.1).

As a result of these changes of bases in X and Y the transformation originally represented by A obtains a new representation, which we will show to be D. We have

$$y' = U^T y = U^T A x = U^T A(Vx')$$

$$= (U^T AV)x' = Dx'.$$

Thus $y' = Dx'$, as was to be proved.

In the new orthogonal coordinate systems the transformation has a very simple representation. In terms of components we have

$$(3.2) \qquad \left\{ \begin{array}{l} y_1' = \mu_1 x_1' \\ y_2' = \mu_2 x_2' \\ \quad \cdot \\ \quad \cdot \\ \quad \cdot \\ y_r' = \mu_r x_r' \\ y_{r+1}' = 0 \\ \quad \cdot \\ \quad \cdot \\ \quad \cdot \\ y_n' = 0. \end{array} \right.$$

The transformation now merely maps the first coordinate axis of X onto the first coordinate axis of Y, with a magnification factor $\mu_1 > 0$. It does the same for the 2nd, 3rd, $\ldots$, r-th coordinate axes of X, with the respective magnification factors $\mu_2, \ldots, \mu_r$. The $(r + 1)$-th, $\ldots$, n-th coordinate axes of X are mapped onto the zero vector of Y.

Let A^T be the transpose of A. Then

$$D^T D = (U^T AV)^T (U^T AV) = V^T A^T U U^T AV = V^T A^T AV.$$

Thus $V^T (A^T A)V = D^T D$, a diagonal matrix with diagonal elements $\mu_1^2, \ldots,$ $\mu_r^2, 0, \ldots, 0$. Since V is orthogonal, $V^T = V^{-1}$, and the transformation $V^T (A^T A)V$ preserves the eigenvalues of $A^T A$, which are therefore $\mu_1^2, \ldots, \mu_n^2$.

Thus the singular values of A are the nonnegative square roots of the eigenvalues of $A^T A$. This last property is frequently used to define these singular values.

From (3.2) we can show that D maps the unit sphere $S = \{x' : \|x'\| = 1\}$ into an r-dimensional hyperellipsoid $E = DS$ of vectors y' such that

$$\frac{y_1'^2}{\mu_1^2} + \cdots + \frac{y_r'^2}{\mu_r^2} = 1 \quad \text{and} \quad y_{r+1} = \cdots = y_n = 0.$$

One of the points of E furthest from the origin θ is the point $(\mu_1, 0, \ldots, 0)$. If $r < n$, then E contains the origin θ. If $r = n$, then E does not contain the origin and one of the points of E closest to θ is $(0, \ldots, 0, \mu_n)$. If $r < n$, then D and hence A are singular matrices. If $r = n$, D and A are nonsingular and have inverses; then directly from (3.2) we see that

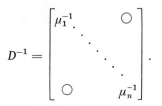

$$D^{-1} = \begin{bmatrix} \mu_1^{-1} & & & \bigcirc \\ & \ddots & & \\ & & \ddots & \\ \bigcirc & & & \mu_n^{-1} \end{bmatrix}.$$

Thus the singular values of A^{-1} are $\mu_1^{-1}, \ldots, \mu_n^{-1}$.

From the discussion above and from (2.6) we see that

(3.3) $\|A\| = \|D\| = \mu_1.$

If $r = n$, then

(3.4) $\|A^{-1}\| = \|D^{-1}\| = \mu_n^{-1}.$

To summarize the most important points for a nonsingular square matrix A with singular values $\mu_1 \geq \cdots \geq \mu_n > 0$: there is one line L_1 in X such that A stretches (or shrinks) L_1 by the factor μ_1 as L_1 is mapped into a line AL_1 of Y. There is a second line L_n, orthogonal to L_1, such that A stretches (or shrinks) L_n by the factor μ_n. Moreover, AL_1 and AL_n are orthogonal in Y. A unit circle in the plane of L_1 and L_n is mapped by A into an ellipse with semiaxes μ_1 and μ_n. This is the greatest distortion which can occur to any circle in X.

Note that the determinant of A, $\det(A)$, satisfies the condition

$$|\det(A)| = \mu_1 \mu_2 \cdots \mu_n.$$

The proof follows from theorem (3.1), the fact that

$$\det(A) = \det(U^T) \cdot \det(D) \cdot \det(V),$$

and the fact that the determinant of an orthogonal matrix is 1 or -1.

(3.5) **Exercise.** If A is a symmetric matrix, prove that in theorem (3.1) the singular values μ_i are the numbers $|\lambda_i|$ taken in the proper order, where the λ_i's are the eigenvalues of A.

4. PROOF OF DIAGONAL-FORM THEOREM

To prove (3.1), note that $B = AA^T$ is a symmetric matrix. Moreover, since for all vectors x,

$$x^T B x = x^T A A^T x = (A^T x)^T (A^T x) = y^T y = \|y\|^2 \geq 0,$$

where $y = A^T x$, we see that B is a positive semidefinite matrix. It follows that all its n eigenvalues are nonnegative, so we may call them $\mu_1^2, \mu_2^2, \ldots, \mu_n^2$, where

$$\mu_1 \geq \mu_2 \geq \cdots \geq \mu_n \geq 0.$$

Assume that $\mu_r > 0$ but that either $r = n$ or $\mu_{r+1} = \cdots = \mu_n = 0$.

Recall from the eigenvalue theory for real symmetric matrices that we can find an orthogonal matrix U so that

$$U^T B U = D^2,$$

where D is a diagonal matrix with diagonal elements

$$d_{i,i} = \mu_i \geq 0 \qquad (i = 1, 2, \ldots, n).$$

Now define the n-by-n matrix F as

(4.1) $$F = U^T A.$$

Then $FF^T = (U^T A)(A^T U) = D^2$. That is,

(4.2) $$FF^T = D^2,$$

a diagonal matrix. The (i, i)-th element of the equality (4.2) states that the norm of the i-th row f_i of F is μ_i ($i = 1, 2, \ldots, n$). That is, $\|f_i\| = \mu_i$. Moreover, the off-diagonal elements of (4.2) state that distinct rows of F are orthogonal to each other. Since $\mu_1 \geq \mu_2 \geq \cdots \geq \mu_r > 0$, the first r rows of F are nonzero, mutually orthogonal vectors $f_1, \ldots, f_r$. If $r < n$, the remaining rows $f_{r+1}, \ldots, f_n$ are the null vector θ.

We now create an orthonormal set of row vectors $v_1, \ldots, v_n$ as follows:

(4.3) $$\text{for } i = 1, \ldots, r, \text{ let } v_i = (1/\mu_i) \cdot f_i.$$

9

Hence $\|v_1\| = \cdots = \|v_r\| = 1$. For $i = r+1, \ldots, n$, choose vectors v_i of norm 1 so that the vectors $v_1, \ldots, v_n$ are mutually orthogonal. This process of completing an orthogonal basis is proved in linear algebra to be always possible.

Let V^T be the matrix whose rows are the vectors $v_1, \ldots, v_n$:

$$V^T = \begin{bmatrix} v_1 \\ \cdot \\ \cdot \\ \cdot \\ v_n \end{bmatrix}.$$

Then the orthonormality of the vectors $\{v_i\}$ means that $V^T V = I$, so that V is an orthogonal matrix. Moreover, we see from (4.3) and above that

$$f_i = \mu_i v_i \quad (i = 1, \ldots, n).$$

Hence

(4.4) $$F = DV^T.$$

But from (4.1) and (4.4)

$$U^T A = DV^T,$$

whence $$U^T A V = D,$$

and thus (3.1) is proved.

Theorem (3.1) can be extended with little change to an arbitrary rectangular matrix A. For completeness we state the result:

(4.5) **Theorem.** *Given any real n-rowed and k-columned matrix A of rank r, there exist an n-by-n real orthogonal matrix U and a k-by-k real orthogonal matrix V so that $U^T A V$ is an n-rowed and k-columned matrix of form*

$$D = \begin{bmatrix} \mu_1 & & & & & \bigcirc \\ & \mu_2 & & & & \\ & & \cdot & & & \\ & & & \cdot & & \\ & & & & \mu_r & \\ \bigcirc & & & & & \end{bmatrix},$$

where $\mu_1 \geq \mu_2 \geq \cdots \geq \mu_r > 0$.

(4.6) **Exercise.** Prove (4.5). *Hint:* Follow the proof for (3.1). Let

$$U^T A A^T U = \begin{bmatrix} D & \Theta \\ \Theta & \Theta \end{bmatrix} \quad \text{and} \quad U^T A = \begin{bmatrix} F \\ G \end{bmatrix}.$$

Show that $G = \Theta$, etc.

(4.7) **Exercise.** Given an arbitrary nonsingular matrix A, find the distance to the closest singular matrix—i.e., find the minimum value of $\|A - S\|$ for singular matrices S. (Answer: μ_n.) Is the closest singular matrix unique?

(4.8) **Exercise.** Given an arbitrary singular matrix A, find the distance to the closest nonsingular matrix.

5. TYPES OF COMPUTATIONAL PROBLEMS IN LINEAR ALGEBRA

We shall first quickly survey the types of problems considered in this book and related problems, and then discuss them in detail. The computational problems of linear algebra include:

a. To solve a linear system $Ax = b$, where A is a given nonsingular square matrix of order n (real or perhaps complex), b is a given column vector of n components, and x is an unknown column vector of n components.

b. In the above problem there are sometimes several different right-hand sides b—for example, k of them—and therefore also k unknown vectors x to be found. If we let B be the n-rowed, k-columned matrix of right-hand sides, and let X be the corresponding n-rowed, k-columned matrix of solution vectors, then we are to solve the linear system $AX = B$, where A is as in **a**.

c. To find the inverse A^{-1} of a given nonsingular matrix A.

d. Given a real symmetric matrix A, to find some or all of its (necessarily real) eigenvalues and sometimes also the corresponding eigenvectors x.

Occasionally A is a complex hermitian matrix (i.e., A is equal to the transpose of its own complex conjugate), and the same problem is posed. In this case each eigenvalue λ is real, but the eigenvectors x will ordinarily be complex.

e. Given a real symmetric matrix A and a real, symmetric, positive definite matrix C, to find some or all of the generalized eigenvalues. A *generalized eigenvalue* is a number λ such that there exists a vector x with $Ax = \lambda Cx$. Perhaps the corresponding vectors x are also to be computed.

f. Given a general real (or even complex) matrix A, to find some or all of the eigenvalues λ of A, and perhaps also the relevant eigenvectors or principal vectors. (Even for real A, all λ may be complex.)

Recall that for each distinct eigenvalue λ of A there exists at least one eigenvector x so that $Ax = \lambda x$. If λ is of algebraic multiplicity m higher than one, eigenvectors corresponding to λ and linearly independent of x may or may not exist. If x is the only eigenvector belonging to λ, there exist so-called

12

principal vectors $y_1, \ldots, y_{m-1}$ (not unique) so that

$$(5.1) \quad \left\{ \begin{array}{l} Ax = \lambda x \\ Ay_1 = \lambda y_1 + x \\ Ay_k = \lambda y_k + y_{k-1} \quad (k = 2, \ldots, m-1). \end{array} \right.$$

The general case is complicated and is governed by the blocks of the Jordan canonical form of A corresponding to the eigenvalue λ.

g. Occasionally, we are to find some or all λ for which

$$\lambda^2 Ax + \lambda Bx + Cx = 0$$

has a solution vector x, where A, B, C are given square matrices. When A and C are singular, the problem is considerably more difficult.

h. Given an n-rowed and k-columned matrix C, where $n > k$, and a column vector d with n components, to find a column vector x with k components so that the norm $\|Cx - d\|$ of the residual vector $Cx - d$ is as small as possible. Such a vector x is a *least-squares solution* of the (usually) inconsistent system of equations $Cx = d$. Unless the rank of C is k, there will be an infinite number of least-squares solution vectors x. Sometimes, we are to find the least-squares solution vector x which has the shortest norm $\|x\|$. This will always be unique.

i. There are a large number of problems dealing with linear inequalities of the form $Ax \geq b$ where the inequality is to be true for each component. One type is: given an n-rowed, k-columned matrix A $(n > k)$, an n-rowed column vector b, and a k-rowed column vector c, find a k-rowed column vector x so that $Ax \geq b$ and $x \geq 0$ and so that $c^T x$ is made as small as possible. Because these problems require quite different attacks and for historical reasons, we will not discuss them here. They are treated in textbooks on linear programming, like Dantzig (1963).

(5.2) **Exercise.** Use the diagonal-form theorem (3.1) to prove the statements made in **h**—i.e., that if the rank is less than k there are an infinite number of least-squares solutions x, but that the shortest one is unique.

(5.3) **Exercise.** Show that in (5.1) we can always choose $x, y_1, \ldots, y_{m-1}$ to be mutually orthogonal vectors.

6. TYPES OF MATRICES ENCOUNTERED IN PRACTICAL PROBLEMS

A square matrix A of order n consists of n^2 elements $a_{i,j}$. When only a few of the elements $a_{i,j}$ are not zero, the matrix is *sparse*. Clearly it can, with appropriate coding, be represented by far fewer than n^2 real numbers since the zero elements need not be stored. A matrix with most of its elements nonzero is a *dense* matrix. The word *density* is used to denote the proportion of nonzero elements.

Sometimes even though no element of a matrix is zero, the elements $a_{i,j}$ can be generated by a simple algorithm depending on the arguments i, j. Such a matrix is a *generated* matrix, and its elements do not require n^2 real numbers of computer storage. If, on the other hand, the elements of a matrix are represented as n^2 real numbers, it is a *stored* matrix. It does not matter whether some elements are zero or not since the zeros will in any event be stored.

One might devise a more subtle measure of the difficulty of representing a matrix based on a quantitative measure of the complexity of the algorithm for generating the matrix. Such a measure of the *informational content* of a matrix might be based crudely on the number of storage cells required for the reconstruction of all elements $a_{i,j}$. Thus a stored matrix would require approximately n^2 cells, whereas a matrix defined, for example, by a simple formula like

$$a_{i,j} = 1/(i + j - 1) \quad (i, j = 1, \dots, n)$$

would require only a few cells. We shall not pursue this matter further.

The orders n of matrices encountered in practice vary enormously, from one up to many thousands. George Dantzig speaks of linear programming problems with a million inequalities on 40,000 unknowns. Varga (1962) mentions having solved linear equation systems with 108,000 unknowns at Bettis Atomic Power Laboratory. Undoubtedly larger equation systems are being solved. Obviously the difficulty of representing a matrix with very large n depends crucially on its density or at least on its informational content. If a matrix must be completely stored, there are two critical sizes. One is determined by the capacity of the rapid-access storage, currently usually made from magnetic cores, and the other by the capacity of the backing storage. Machines with 32,000 words of rapid-access storage restrict n to perhaps 150 since usually several thousand words are needed for residual programs. If n^2 exceeds the size of rapid-access storage, backing storage (drums, tapes, disks) must be used, with substantial problems of organizing transfers between the principal and the backing stores, with proper timing, buffering, and so on. With backing storage, dense matrices of orders up to around 1000 can be handled. And, indeed, the practical limitation for matrix operations is more likely to be the operation time than the time for transferring data. (If magnetic tapes are used to invert a dense matrix of order 1000, the tapes are likely to wear so much that they become unreadable before the inversion is accomplished!) Once n substantially exceeds 1000, it is essential that the matrix be sparse.

Algorithms for solving the various computational problems of linear algebra differ according to whether they alter the matrix data or leave them alone. The most suitable methods for small, stored matrices generally do alter the matrices. However, such methods, when applied to sparse matrices, will usually increase the density of the matrices as they proceed. Hence, if a matrix is of high order and also sparse, it is not generally possible to use the methods best suited to small, stored matrices.

A is said to be a *band matrix* if $a_{i,j} = 0$ for $|i - j| > m$ because the nonzero elements form a band along the main diagonal; the number of diagonals in the band is $2m + 1$. See Sec. 23. Band matrices occur in situations in which each unknown quantity is coupled to only a few of the others. Examples include a system of equations describing an electrical network involving many components but relatively few interconnections, and a finite-difference approximation to an ordinary or partial differential equation.

(6.1)   **Definition.**   A matrix A is *diagonally dominant* if

(6.2) $$|a_{i,i}| \geq \sum_{j \neq i} |a_{i,j}| \qquad \text{for all } i,$$

with inequality for at least one i.

(6.3)   **Definition.**   A matrix A is *reducible* if there exist a permutation of the rows and an (ordinarily different) permutation of the columns so that the resulting rearrangement of A takes the form

$$\begin{bmatrix} B & \Theta \\ C & D \end{bmatrix},$$

where B and D are square submatrices and Θ is a zero matrix.

(6.4)   **Definition.**   A matrix A is *irreducible* if it is not reducible.

(6.5)   **Exercise.**   Prove that a diagonally dominant and irreducible matrix cannot be singular. (For a partial solution see the Appendix.)

(6.6)   **Research problem.**   Write an efficient computer program to determine whether or not a given stored matrix is reducible.

7. SOURCES OF COMPUTA-
TIONAL PROBLEMS OF
LINEAR ALGEBRA

Referring to the outline in Sec. 5, we shall indicate some sources of the computational problems of linear algebra.

The solution of systems of linear algebraic equations, problem **a**, is perhaps the most frequently encountered problem in a computing center. The applied mathematician is frequently in the position of choosing parameters to fit data. For example, he may be trying to interpolate n given function values by a polynomial with n coefficient parameters. Since the coefficients of a polynomial influence the value of the polynomial linearly, this interpolation problem results in a linear algebraic system. In more complicated problems where the parameters do not enter linearly, the equations are nonlinear. However, a typical way to solve a nonlinear system of equations is to linearize them and then to solve the linearized system—again a problem of type **a**.

The most common source of linear equation systems is the approximation of a continuous functional equation by a finite-difference problem. For example, one may approximate the Dirichlet problem for Laplace's differential operator by a large system of simple finite-difference equations in two dimensions. (See Sec. 24.) The matrices associated with difference equations are almost always large and sparse.

A second very substantial source of linear equation systems is the solution of a linear least-squares problem. In **h** of Sec. 5 suppose that C has the full rank k. We shall prove below that $C^T C$ is also of rank k and hence is nonsingular and positive definite. Then the problem is to minimize

$$
\begin{aligned}
\|Cx - d\|^2 &= (Cx - d)^T(Cx - d) \\
&= x^T C^T C x - 2x^T C^T d + d^T d \\
&= (C^T C x - C^T d)^T (C^T C)^{-1} (C^T C x - C^T d) \\
&\quad - d^T C(C^T C)^{-1} C^T d + d^T d.
\end{aligned}
$$

(7.1)

The reader can verify these equalities by multiplication. Since $(C^T C)^{-1}$ is positive definite, the minimum in (7.1) is achieved when $C^T C x - C^T d = 0$, i.e., when x satisfies the so-called *normal equations*

$$
C^T C x = C^T d.
$$

This presents a problem of type **a** in Sec. 5.

To show that $C^T C$ is of rank k we will prove the more general result that

(7.2)   the rank of $C^T C$ is equal to the rank of C.

We use the result (4.5) that there exist orthogonal matrices U, V so that

(7.3) $U^T C V = D$.

We now see that $C = U D V^T$, so that

$$C^T C = (V D^T U^T) U D V^T = V D^T D V^T.$$

But clearly $D^T D$ and D have the same rank r. Thus $C^T C$ and C have the same rank.

The linear equation systems coming from normal equations are typically of small order and dense. Although it is common, the use of the normal equations is often not the most efficient or accurate method for solving least-squares problems. See Golub (1965), Businger and Golub (1965), and Golub and Kahan (1965).

Frequently the problems leading to linear equation systems occur in sets, characterized by the same functional relations but different data. For example, a finite-difference equation system can have several sets of boundary conditions for the same "interior" equations. Or a least-squares fitting problem can be provided with several sets of data vectors d for one set of governing parameters C. These situations lead to linear systems of form $AX = B$, i.e., problem **b**.

We will see below in connection with iterative improvement that sometimes the different columns of the matrix B will occur at different times in a solution process. For example, the second column b_2 may be computed from the first column b_1.

Inverting a matrix, problem **c**, is most apt to be needed in statistical computations, where the inverse has importance in itself as an estimate of certain statistical parameters. In most other practical problems the inverse is not really needed, although there may be great interest in its norm.

If there are many different right-hand sides b for a given matrix A, the inverse A^{-1} in fact represents the "influence operator" which directly converts b into the solution x of the system $Ax = b$; i.e., $x = A^{-1}b$. For this reason one is frequently asked to provide A^{-1} just so a new b can be converted into x by the multiplication $A^{-1}b$. However, if A is a sparse matrix, the inverse A^{-1} is normally a dense matrix. So, although A can be stored in a small space, the inverse A^{-1} will usually require a prohibitive amount of storage. Fortunately, there are often ways to store data from which $A^{-1}b$ can be quickly computed from b, without having to store the elements of

A^{-1} and with less rounding error than arises from the multiplication of A^{-1} by b. See Sec. 18.

Problems **f** and **g** typically arise in the solution of a coupled system of linear, homogeneous ordinary differential equations with constant co-efficients. If we represent such a system in the form $dz/dt = Az$, where $z = z(t)$ is an n-dimensional vector, the attempt to find an exponential solution in the form $z(t) = x \cdot \exp(\lambda t)$, where x is a constant n vector, leads directly to problem **f** for the determination of λ.

In the same way, the second-order system

$$(7.4) \qquad A\frac{d^2z}{dt^2} + B\frac{dz}{dt} + Cz = \theta$$

leads to problem **g**. It is particularly common in the study of nonconservative dynamical systems, like servos, where energy is being introduced and one cannot be sure that the systems will be stable.

In electrical problems leading to systems of type (7.4), A is frequently the matrix of inductances, B is the matrix of resistances, and C is the matrix of admittances. In analogous mechanical systems, A is the matrix of masses or inertias, B is the matrix of resistance coefficients, and C is the matrix which provides the forces.

In many problems $B = \Theta$, and A and C are symmetric, positive definite matrices. Then the system (7.4) takes the form

$$(7.5) \qquad A\frac{d^2z}{dt^2} + Cz = \theta.$$

Let $z(t) = x \cdot \exp(i\omega t)$, where x is a constant vector and ω is a frequency of resonant vibration of the system. We are then led to the system

$$-\omega^2 Ax + Cx = \theta,$$

or, letting $\lambda = 1/\omega^2$, we have

$$(7.6) \qquad Ax = \lambda Cx,$$

which is problem **e** of Sec. 5. Thus problem **e** usually corresponds to the determination of the frequencies of vibration of a conservative dynamical system.

In many particular cases the mass matrix A is the identity. Then one usually lets $\lambda = \omega^2$ and gets the ordinary eigenvalue problem **d**:

$$(7.7) \qquad Cx = \lambda x,$$

where C is a positive definite matrix.

Another source of problems of type **d** is a part of the factor-analysis problem. Here one is given a symmetric positive semidefinite (correlation) matrix R of order n, and as part of the complete factor analysis one seeks to represent R as well as possible in the form ff^T, where f is a column vector to be found. Let the i, j, element of R be denoted $r_{i,j}$. That of ff^T is $f_i f_j$. Then we seek f so that

$$\sum_{i,j=1}^{n} (r_{i,j} - f_i f_j)^2 = \text{minimum.}$$

A short calculation shows that the minimum occurs for some vector f such that Rf is a multiple of f. That is, f is an eigenvector of R. A further calculation shows that, if the eigenvalues of R are

$$\lambda_1 \geq \lambda_2 \geq \ldots \geq \lambda_n \geq 0,$$

with corresponding eigenvectors $u_1, \ldots, u_n$, then the best choice of f is $\sqrt{\lambda_1}\, u_1$. Thus, omitting details, we claim that this part of factor analysis leads to an eigenvalue problem for real symmetric matrices—problem **d**.

(7.8) **Exercise.** Prove the statements just made about f.

In this book we confine ourselves to the numerical solution of problems of types **a**, **b**, and **c**.

8. CONDITION OF A LINEAR SYSTEM

Consider the equation system $Ax = b$, where A is a nonsingular matrix of order n; i.e., $\det (A) \neq 0$ or, equivalently, all $\mu_i > 0$ in (3.1). Since such a matrix represents a 1–1 mapping of R^n onto R^n, it has a unique inverse. That is, the system has a unique solution x which we may write in the form $A^{-1}b$.

Let us suppose that the data (the numbers in A and b) are subject to uncertainty and that we want to know what effect this uncertainty has on the solution vector x. To start, suppose that A is known exactly but that the vector b is subject to uncertainty. For example, $b + \delta b$ is another right-hand side close to b and $A(x + \delta x) = b + \delta b$. Let us see how large δx can be. We have

$$\delta x = A^{-1}\,\delta b.$$

Hence

$$(8.1) \qquad \|\delta x\| \leq \|A^{-1}\| \cdot \|\delta b\|,$$

and equality is possible for certain vectors δb. Since $b = Ax$, we have

$$(8.2) \qquad \|b\| \leq \|A\| \cdot \|x\|.$$

Multiply (8.1) by (8.2):

$$(8.3) \qquad \|\delta x\| \cdot \|b\| \leq \|A\| \cdot \|A^{-1}\| \cdot \|x\| \cdot \|\delta b\|.$$

Assuming only that $b \neq \theta$, we find from (8.3) that

$$(8.4) \qquad \frac{\|\delta x\|}{\|x\|} \leq \|A\| \cdot \|A^{-1}\| \cdot \frac{\|\delta b\|}{\|b\|}.$$

For any nonsingular matrix A we define the *condition number* of A, denoted by cond (A), to be the number $\|A\| \cdot \|A^{-1}\|$. (Thus actually the condition number depends on the norm used.) For the euclidean norm, recall from (3.3) and (3.4) that

$$(8.5) \qquad \text{cond}\,(A) = \|A\| \cdot \|A^{-1}\| = \mu_1/\mu_n \geq 1,$$

where μ_1, μ_n are the largest and smallest singular values of A, respectively. Thus cond (A) is a measure of the maximum distortion which the linear transformation with matrix A makes on the unit sphere. We have from (8.4) that

$$(8.6) \qquad \frac{\|\delta x\|}{\|x\|} \leq \text{cond}\,(A)\,\frac{\|\delta b\|}{\|b\|}.$$

Now $\|\delta b\|/\|b\|$ can be interpreted as a measure of the relative uncertainty in the data vector b. If the elements of b are known to five significant decimals, for example, then $\|\delta b\|/\|b\|$ is around 10^{-4} or 10^{-5}. In the same way, $\|\delta x\|/\|x\|$ can be interpreted as the relative uncertainty in the solution vector x, which is due to the uncertainty in b. The meaning of (8.6), then, is that cond (A) bounds the ratio of the relative uncertainty of the solution x to that of the given b. Since cond $(A) \geq 1$, by (8.5), we see that this bound is never less than one.

We wish to emphasize the fact that, for appropriate choices of the directions of b and δb, there can be equality in (8.1) and (8.2), so that equality is possible also in (8.6). Thus no sharper bound than (8.6) can be given for arbitrary vectors b and δb, no matter how large or small $\|b\|$ and $\|\delta b\|$ are. Because it is crucially important that the reader understand the reason for this, we shall demonstrate why equality can occur in (8.1), (8.2), and (8.6). We use theorem (3.1) to show the existence of U, V so that $U^T A V = D$. Then, as in Sec. 3, we introduce orthogonal coordinate transformations in the space X of x and in the space Y of right-hand sides b, so that the equation $Ax = b$ becomes

$$(8.7) \qquad Dx' = b',$$

or

$$(8.8) \qquad \begin{cases} \mu_1 x_1' = b_1' \\ \mu_2 x_2' = b_2' \\ \cdot \\ \cdot \\ \cdot \\ \mu_n x_n' = b_n'. \end{cases}$$

At the same time, the equation $A(\delta x) = \delta b$ for the uncertainties becomes, in the new coordinate systems,

$$(8.9) \qquad D\,\delta x' = \delta b',$$

or

$$(8.10) \qquad \begin{cases} \mu_1\,\delta x_1' = \delta b_1' \\ \mu_2\,\delta x_2' = \delta b_2' \\ \cdot \\ \cdot \\ \cdot \\ \mu_n\,\delta x_n' = \delta b_n'. \end{cases}$$

Since $\mu_1 \geq \mu_2 \geq \cdots \geq \mu_n > 0$, $\|A\| = \|D\| = \mu_1$, and $\|A^{-1}\| = \|D^{-1}\| = \mu_n^{-1}$, we shall see how equalities are possible in (8.1), (8.2), and (8.6). Suppose $b' = (\beta, 0, \ldots, 0)^T$, so that $b_1' = \beta$ but $b_i' = 0$ ($i \geq 2$). Then

$$x' = (\mu_1^{-1}\beta, 0, \ldots, 0)^T,$$

and we have equality in (8.2) no matter what nonzero constant β is. On the other hand, suppose $\delta b' = (0, \ldots, 0, \gamma)^T$, so that $\delta b_1' = 0, \ldots, \delta b_{n-1}' = 0$, $\delta b_n' = \gamma$. Then

$$\delta x' = (0, \ldots, 0, \mu_n^{-1}\gamma)^T,$$

and we have equality in (8.1) no matter how large or small the nonzero constant γ is.

In short, we get equality in (8.6) if the right side b is in a direction which receives the greatest magnification by A (and thus the least magnification by A^{-1}) and if the perturbation δb is in a direction which receives the least magnification by A (and thus the greatest magnification by A^{-1}). These two directions are necessarily orthogonal, as long as $\mu_1 \neq \mu_n$. The condition number cond (A) is invariant when A is multiplied by a constant, and it is a reasonably good measure of the badness of A with respect to the computations involved in equation solving. Note that cond $(A) =$ cond (A^{-1}).

If cond $(A) = 1$, then A and A^{-1} stretch all directions alike since $\mu_1 = \mu_2 = \cdots = \mu_n$, and it is impossible for A^{-1} to stretch δb any more than b. Then $\|\delta x\|$ bears the same ratio to $\|x\|$ that $\|\delta b\|$ does to $\|b\|$. The relative uncertainty in x is thus precisely the same as that of b. However, if cond (A) is 10^6, then A^{-1} stretches one direction a million times as much as another direction. If b gets the short stretch, and δb gets the long stretch, then it is clear that $\|\delta x\|/\|x\|$ will be a million times $\|\delta b\|/\|b\|$. If cond (A) is relatively small, A is *well conditioned* (with respect to the linear equations problem). If cond (A) is relatively large, than A is *badly conditioned* or *ill conditioned* (with respect to this problem).

A popular misconception is that the smallness of det (A) causes the ill condition of A. Our considerations have shown that this is not so. For, if

$$\mu_1 = \mu_2 = \cdots = \mu_n = 10^{-30},$$

then det $(A) = 10^{-30n}$, a very small number, but the relative error $\|\delta x\|/\|x\|$ is precisely equal to $\|\delta b\|/\|b\|$. If μ_1 and n are fixed, it is true that det $(A) \to 0$ implies that $\mu_n \to 0$ and hence that cond $(A) \to \infty$. Thus, the smallness of det (A) bears some relation to the ill condition of a matrix A of fixed order n as long as we somehow normalize A so that μ_1 remains fixed. To see how weak this relation can be, however, suppose that n is 101, $\mu_1 = 1$, and $\mu_2 = \cdots = \mu_n = 10^{-1}$. Then det $(A) = \mu_1\mu_2^{n-1} = 10^{-100}$, whereas cond $(A) = \mu_1\mu_2^{-1} = 10$. Thus A is very well conditioned, although its determinant is quite small.

In the preceding discussion we assumed that A was known precisely but that b was subject to uncertainty, and found that cond (A) was a critical measure. It turns out that cond (A) is equally important when A is subject to uncertainty, even though b is known exactly. In fact, if $x = A^{-1}b$ and

$$(8.11) \qquad\qquad x + \delta x = (A + \delta A)^{-1}b,$$

then we see that

$$(8.12) \qquad\qquad \delta x = [(A + \delta A)^{-1} - A^{-1}]b.$$

Setting $A + \delta A = B$ in the interesting identity

$$(8.13) \qquad\qquad B^{-1} - A^{-1} = A^{-1}(A - B)B^{-1},$$

we see from (8.12) that

$$(8.14) \qquad \delta x = -A^{-1}(\delta A)(A + \delta A)^{-1}b = -A^{-1}(\delta A)(x + \delta x).$$

Taking norms in (8.14), we obtain

$$\|\delta x\| \leq \|A^{-1}\| \cdot \|\delta A\| \cdot \|x + \delta x\|.$$

It follows finally that

$$(8.15) \qquad\qquad \frac{\|\delta x\|}{\|x + \delta x\|} \leq \text{cond}\,(A)\,\frac{\|\delta A\|}{\|A\|}.$$

Thus the uncertainty in x, taken relative to $x + \delta x$, is bounded by the relative uncertainty of A multiplied by cond (A). There is no approximation in (8.15).

(8.16) **Exercise.** Show that, if $\|\delta A\|/\|A\|$ is small enough,

$$\frac{\|\delta x\|}{\|x\|} \leq \text{cond}\,(A)\,\frac{\|\delta A\|}{\|A\|} \quad \text{(approximately)}.$$

(8.17) **Exercise.** Recall that the differential dx is the linear part of δx as a function of the elements of the matrix δA. Prove that

$$\frac{\|dx\|}{\|x\|} \leq \text{cond}\,(A)\,\frac{\|\delta A\|}{\|A\|} \quad \text{(exactly)}.$$

(8.18) **Exercise.**   Prove that

$$\frac{\|B^{-1} - A^{-1}\|}{\|B^{-1}\|} \leq \text{cond}(A)\,\frac{\|A - B\|}{\|A\|},$$

an inequality showing how little $\|B^{-1} - A^{-1}\|$ is in terms of $\|A - B\|$. The inequality was used by Bauer (1960) to motivate the definition of cond (A).

Note that we have not referred to rounding errors in the discussion so far. We have merely been discussing the inherent uncertainty in the solution of a linear system due to uncertainties in the data. This sensitivity of the answers to the data provides the problem with a built-in noise level; there is no use attributing much accuracy to solutions x which are expressed to more precision than the inherent uncertainty warrants. In fact, as shown in Secs. 20 and 21, we like to express rounding error in terms of uncertainty in the data, so that rounding error can indeed be studied in terms of cond (A).

It is important to realize that cond (A) can be enormous—even in simple problems!

(8.19) **Exercise.**   If A is orthogonal, prove that cond $(A) = 1$, no matter how large n is.

(8.20) **Example.**   Let

$$A = \begin{bmatrix} 1 & .99 \\ .99 & .98 \end{bmatrix}.$$

Then $\lambda_2 \doteq -0.00005$, $\lambda_1 \doteq 1.98005$. Since $A = A^T$, $A^T A = A^2$ has eigenvalues $(0.00005)^2$, $(1.98005)^2$. Then $\mu_2 \doteq 0.00005$, $\mu_1 \doteq 1.98005$, and cond $(A) \doteq 39,600$. Thus A distorts the plane enormously, and we expect grave trouble. To continue, consider the system

$$\begin{cases} x_1 + .99x_2 = 1.99 \\ .99x_1 + .98x_2 = 1.97. \end{cases}$$

The true solution is $x_1 = 1$, $x_2 = 1$. But $x_1 = 3.0000$, $x_2 = -1.0203$ yield

$$\begin{cases} x_1 + .99x_2 = 1.989903 \\ .99x_1 + .98x_2 = 1.970106. \end{cases}$$

Thus a change $\delta b = \begin{bmatrix} -.000097 \\ +.000106 \end{bmatrix}$ gives $\delta x = \begin{bmatrix} +2.0000 \\ -2.0203 \end{bmatrix}$. Since

$\|\delta x\| \doteq 2\sqrt{2} \doteq 2.82$ and $\|x\| = \sqrt{2}$, we have $\|\delta x\|/\|x\| \doteq 2$ and $\|\delta b\| \doteq$
$10^{-4}\sqrt{2}$, $\|b\| \doteq 2\sqrt{2}$, $\|\delta b\|/\|b\| \doteq 10^{-4}/2$. Hence $\|\delta x\|/\|x\| \doteq 40,000 \cdot$
$\|\delta b\|/\|b\|$. Since cond $(A) \doteq 39,600$, we have found approximately the
worst case. If the vector b is known with an uncertainty of about
0.0001 in its components, then the vector x can only be known to
within about 2 in its components. This is a very ill conditioned
problem because the two lines whose intersection we seek are
practically coincident.

It is worth stressing again that the size of cond (A) is a far more important criterion of the badness of a linear system $Ax = b$ than either the
smallness of det (A) or the largeness of the order n.

If it is known that $\|A\|$ is 1, then obviously cond (A) is equal to $\|A^{-1}\|$.
In cruder terms, if the elements of A are roughly in the range 0.1 to 1.0, then
the condition of A is of the general size of the elements of A^{-1}. Thus, if a
matrix is prescaled so that its elements are near 1, a sure manifestation of the
ill condition of A is that some or all elements of A^{-1} are large.

(8.21) **Exercise.** If $A = \begin{bmatrix} a & b \\ c & d \end{bmatrix}$ is nonsingular, define

$$\sigma = \frac{a^2 + b^2 + c^2 + d^2}{2|ad - bc|}.$$

Prove that cond $(A) = \sigma + \sqrt{\sigma^2 - 1}$. (See Appendix for sketch of
solution.)

(8.22) **Exercise.** Prove that

$$\begin{bmatrix} 100 & 99 \\ 99 & 98 \end{bmatrix}$$

and its various permutations are the worst conditioned of the nonsingular matrices of order 2 with elements that are positive integers
≤ 100. (Thus the example (8.20) was hardly a random choice!)

(8.23) **Exercise.** Let A and A^{-1} be as follows:

$$A = \begin{bmatrix} 6 & 13 & -17 \\ 13 & 29 & -38 \\ -17 & -38 & 50 \end{bmatrix} \; ; \quad A^{-1} = \begin{bmatrix} 6 & -4 & -1 \\ -4 & 11 & 7 \\ -1 & 7 & 5 \end{bmatrix}.$$

The eigenvalues of A are approximately

$$\lambda_1 = .0588, \qquad \lambda_2 = .2007, \qquad \lambda_3 = 84.74.$$

(a) Describe the set $S = \{Ax \mid \|x\| = 1\}$, the image under A of the unit sphere. Be sure to give any numbers which describe the size of S.

(b)
$$\|A\| = \; ?$$
$$\|A^{-1}\| = \; ?$$
$$\text{cond}\,(A) = \; ?$$

(c) Consider the equation system $Ax = b$. Suppose we have vectors b and x, about which we know only that

$$\|b - Ax\| \le .01.$$

(i) Precisely how small an upper bound can one give for the absolute error $\|x - A^{-1}b\|$?

(ii) Precisely how small an upper bound can one give for the relative error

$$\|x - A^{-1}b\|/\|A^{-1}b\|?$$

9. GAUSSIAN ELIMINATION AND
LU DECOMPOSITION

For a linear system of equations $Ax = b$ with a dense matrix whose elements are stored in high-speed memory, no class of solution algorithms has been found which is better, either in time or in accuracy, than the systematic elimination methods of C. F. Gauss. It therefore seems that every computer library should have good programs for solving linear systems by elimination. This section explains this class of algorithms and also some particular versions of it.

Gaussian elimination occurs in many variants which are algebraically the same. The methods differ according to how the matrices are stored, the order of the elimination, the precautions taken against large rounding errors, and the way calculated solutions are improved. There are also variants specially adapted for systems with symmetric, positive definite matrices, in which the storage is approximately halved.

(9.1) **Definition.** A *lower triangular* matrix is a square matrix $C = (c_{i,j})$ such that $c_{i,j} = 0$ for $i < j$. Similarly, if $c_{i,j} = 0$ for $i > j$, C is *upper triangular*.

The algebraic basis of Gaussian elimination is the following theorem:

(9.2) **LU Theorem.** *Given a square matrix A of order n, let A_k denote the principal minor matrix made from the first k rows and columns. Assume that $\det (A_k) \neq 0$ for $k = 1, 2, \ldots, n - 1$. Then there exist a unique lower triangular matrix $L = (m_{i,j})$, with $m_{1,1} = m_{2,2} = \cdots = m_{n,n} = 1$, and a unique upper triangular matrix $U = (u_{i,j})$ so that $LU = A$. Moreover, $\det (A) = u_{1,1} u_{2,2} \cdots u_{n,n}$.*

To prove this theorem we use induction on n. If $n = 1$, clearly $a_{1,1} = 1 \cdot u_{1,1}$ uniquely, and $\det (A) = u_{1,1}$. Assume the theorem is true for $n = k - 1$. For $n = k$ we partition A into submatrices:

$$A = \begin{bmatrix} A_{k-1} & c \\ r & a_{k,k} \end{bmatrix},$$

where r is a row of $k - 1$ components and c is a column of $k - 1$ components. Write

$$L = \begin{bmatrix} L_{k-1} & 0 \\ m & 1 \end{bmatrix}, \qquad U = \begin{bmatrix} U_{k-1} & u \\ 0 & u_{k,k} \end{bmatrix}.$$

Then

$$LU = \begin{bmatrix} L_{k-1}U_{k-1} & L_{k-1}u \\ & \\ & \\ mU_{k-1} & mu + u_{k,k} \end{bmatrix}.$$

Now, by the inductive hypothesis, L_{k-1} and U_{k-1} are uniquely determined and $L_{k-1}U_{k-1} = A_{k-1}$. Moreover, neither L_{k-1} nor U_{k-1} is singular (or else A_{k-1} would be singular, contrary to the hypothesis). Then the requirement $LU = A$ is equivalent to $L_{k-1}u = c$ and $mU_{k-1} = r$ and $mu + u_{k,k} = a_{k,k}$. Thus u, m, and $u_{k,k}$ can be determined uniquely in that order, and L and U are determined uniquely. Finally,

$$\det (A) = \det (L) \cdot \det (U)$$

$$= 1 \cdot \det (U_{k-1}) \cdot u_{kk}$$

$$= u_{1,1} \cdot \ldots \cdot u_{k-1,k-1} \cdot u_{k,k},$$

completing the proof of (9.2).

In a similar way one can prove under the same hypotheses that A can be uniquely decomposed in the form $A = LDU$, where L and U are upper and lower triangular matrices with 1's on the diagonal and D is a diagonal matrix. Moreover, $\det (A) = d_{1,1} \cdot \ldots \cdot d_{n,n}$. Actually, the U of the LU theorem is simply the DU of the LDU theorem. Next, one can show that, if A is symmetric and satisfies the hypotheses of the LU theorem, then $A = LDU$ implies that $U = L^T$, the transpose of L. If A is positive definite, then it is a theorem of matrix theory that $\det (A_r) > 0$ for $r = 1, 2, \ldots, n$, and hence in the LDU theorem one has all $d_{r,r} > 0$. If we let

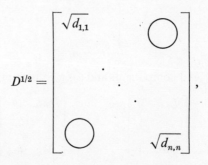

$$D^{1/2} = \begin{bmatrix} \sqrt{d_{1,1}} & & \bigcirc \\ & \cdot & \\ & & \cdot \\ \bigcirc & & \sqrt{d_{n,n}} \end{bmatrix},$$

we can let $G = LD^{1/2}$, and then $A = GG^T$. In summary:

(9.3) **Corollary.** *If A is a symmetric, positive definite matrix, then it can be decomposed uniquely into GG^T, where G is a lower triangular matrix with positive diagonal elements.*

The factorization of A as the product LU is the basic idea of all Gaussian elimination schemes, for then the system $Ax = b$ can be written

$$LUx = b.$$

This represents two triangular systems

$$Ly = b \quad \text{and} \quad Ux = y,$$

which are very easily solved. The components of the intermediate solution y can be obtained directly from the first system since the first equation involves only y_1, the second only y_1 and y_2, and so on. Then the components of x can be similarly obtained from the second system in the order x_n, $x_{n-1}, \ldots, x_1$. The calculation of L and U together with the solution of $Ly = b$ are usually called the *forward elimination*, and the solution of $Ux = y$ is the *back substitution*. We will also refer to the computation of L and U as the *triangular decomposition*.

The various methods differ in the order in which the operations are carried out in the forward elimination. There are important distinctions in whether the equations (rows of A) are interchanged or not, or in whether the variables (columns of A) are interchanged. Interchanges will be discussed in Sec. 10, after we have described elimination in more detail. Also, sometimes the matrix L is stored, and sometimes it is not. The importance of saving L can be demonstrated easily if A is a general stored matrix. The diagonal of L need not be stored since it is known to be all 1's. The below-diagonal part of L together with U can occupy the space originally taken by A. No intermediate storage is needed since elements of L are created at the same time that elements of A are zeroed. Almost all the computer time required to solve $Ax = b$ is spent finding L and U; the computations actually involving b are relatively short. Hence, if one might later need to solve another system with the same matrix A but with a new right-hand side b, there is every reason to retain L and U and thereby avoid repeating the triangular decomposition. New systems with the same A occur, for example, in computing the inverse matrix A^{-1}. They also occur in an iterative improvement of the first solution, a process for finding x to high accuracy, which we shall describe in Sec. 13.

Let us relate the above matrix discussion to ordinary elimination. Given a matrix A and a vector b of order 4, one uses elementary row operations to put zeros below the main diagonal of A. Assume $a_{1,1} \neq 0$. Let $m_{i,1} = a_{i,1}/a_{1,1}$ ($i = 2, 3, 4$). For $i = 2, 3, 4$ one subtracts $m_{i,1}$ times the first equation from the i-th equation, and also subtracts $m_{i,1}$ times b_1 from b_i, to obtain three equations that do not involve x_1. This new set of three equations together with the first equation of the original set can be written

$$A^{(2)}x = b^{(2)},$$

where $A^{(2)} = (a_{i,j}^{(2)})$, and $a_{i,1}^{(2)} = 0$ for $i = 2, 3, 4$. If M_1 is the lower triangular matrix

$$M_1 = \begin{bmatrix} 1 & & & \\ -m_{2,1} & 1 & & \\ -m_{3,1} & 0 & 1 & \\ -m_{4,1} & 0 & 0 & 1 \end{bmatrix},$$

then we have $A^{(2)} = M_1 A, \qquad b^{(2)} = M_1 b.$

Now assume $a_{2,2}^{(2)} \neq 0$. Let $m_{i,2} = a_{i,2}^{(2)}/a_{2,2}^{(2)}$ ($i = 3, 4$). Then premultiply $A^{(2)}$ and $b^{(2)}$ by

$$M_2 = \begin{bmatrix} 1 & & & \\ 0 & 1 & & \\ 0 & -m_{3,2} & 1 & \\ 0 & -m_{4,2} & 0 & 1 \end{bmatrix}$$

to obtain $A^{(3)} = M_2 A^{(2)}$ and $b^{(3)} = M_2 b^{(2)}$. This corresponds to eliminating x_2 from the last two equations. Finally, assume $a_{3,3}^{(3)} \neq 0$, let $m_{4,3} = a_{4,3}^{(3)}/a_{3,3}^{(3)}$, and premultiply $A^{(3)}$ and $b^{(3)}$ by

$$M_3 = \begin{bmatrix} 1 & & & \\ 0 & 1 & & \\ 0 & 0 & 1 & \\ 0 & 0 & -m_{4,3} & 1 \end{bmatrix}.$$

Then $A^{(4)} = M_3 A^{(3)} = M_3 M_2 M_1 A$

is an upper triangular matrix, which we denote by U. The original system now takes the form $Ux = A^{(4)}x = b^{(4)} = M_3 b^{(3)}$, and has the following structure:

(9.4)

$$
\begin{bmatrix}
a_{1,1} & a_{1,2} & a_{1,3} & a_{1,4} \\
 & a_{2,2}^{(2)} & a_{2,3}^{(2)} & a_{2,4}^{(2)} \\
 & & a_{3,3}^{(3)} & a_{3,4}^{(3)} \\
 & & & a_{4,4}^{(4)}
\end{bmatrix}
\begin{bmatrix}
x_1 \\ x_2 \\ x_3 \\ x_4
\end{bmatrix}
=
\begin{bmatrix}
b_1 \\ b_2^{(2)} \\ b_3^{(3)} \\ b_4^{(4)}
\end{bmatrix}.
$$

Let $M = M_3 M_2 M_1$. Then, since $MA = U$, we have $A = M^{-1}U$. But $M^{-1} = M_1^{-1}M_2^{-1}M_3^{-1}$. It is not difficult to see that M_k^{-1} is simply M_k with the signs of its off-diagonal elements reversed. Furthermore, the product $M_1^{-1}M_2^{-1}M_3^{-1}$ is simply

$$
L = M^{-1} =
\begin{bmatrix}
1 & & & \\
m_{2,1} & 1 & & \\
m_{3,1} & m_{3,2} & 1 & \\
m_{4,1} & m_{4,2} & m_{4,3} & 1
\end{bmatrix}.
$$

Hence M^{-1} is the L of the LU theorem; i.e., $A = M^{-1}U = LU$. Note that the matrix M is never actually formed and, in fact, is not easily expressed in terms of $m_{i,j}$. As the elimination progresses, the below-diagonal elements $m_{i,j}$ of L are stored in place of the below-diagonal elements of A, and the elements $u_{i,j}$ of U are stored in place of the diagonal and above-diagonal elements of A. At the end, one has the tableau

$$
\begin{bmatrix}
u_{1,1} & u_{1,2} & u_{1,3} & u_{1,4} \\
m_{2,1} & u_{2,2} & u_{2,3} & u_{2,4} \\
m_{3,1} & m_{3,2} & u_{3,3} & u_{3,4} \\
m_{4,1} & m_{4,2} & m_{4,3} & u_{4,4}
\end{bmatrix}
$$

stored in place of A.

The processing of the right-hand side—that is, the transformation of b into $b^{(4)}$—is often done simultaneously with the processing of A, but, since we save all the necessary multipliers, it can just as well be done later as a separate operation.

The above constitutes ordinary Gaussian elimination without interchanges. Triangular decomposition is summarized by the facts that L is simply the matrix of multipliers $(m_{i,j})$ with a diagonal of 1's and that U is the matrix $A^{(4)}$ of (9.4). Note also that the intermediate solution y is simply $b^{(4)}$, the right-hand side of (9.4).

(9.5)   **Exercise.**   The amount of arithmetic in a matrix algorithm is usually measured by the number of multiplicative operations—i.e., multiplications and divisions—used since there are normally approximately the same number of additive operations. (i) Count the number of multiplicative operations required to solve the n-by-n system $Ax = b$ with Gaussian elimination and show that it is a polynomial in n whose leading term is $\frac{1}{3}n^3$. (ii) How many multiplicative operations are required to solve the system with a new right-hand side, $Ax = b'$, if the triangular decomposition has been saved? (iii) If multiplication and division each take 25 microseconds, how much time do the operations in (i) and (ii) take when one solves a system of order 100? 1000?

(9.6)   **Exercise.**   Recall that Cramer's rule expresses each component of the solution x as the ratio of two n-by-n determinants. Suppose each determinant were evaluated as the sum of $n!$ products of n factors each. How many multiplicative operations would be required here for orders 100 and 1000? How much time?

Klyuyev and Kokovkin-Shcherbak (1965) have proved that no general system of linear algebraic equations can be solved in fewer operations than are required by Gaussian elimination.

(9.7)   **Exercise.**   State and prove a UL theorem analogous to the LU theorem (9.2).

(9.8)   **Exercise.**   If A is a real, symmetric, nonsingular (but possibly indefinite) matrix, prove that

$$A = GDG^T,$$

where G is a lower triangular matrix with positive diagonal elements, and D is a diagonal matrix with all

$$|d_{i,i}| = 1.$$

10. NEED FOR INTERCHANGING ROWS

We assumed that $a_{1,1} \neq 0$, $a_{2,2}^{(2)} \neq 0$, $a_{3,3}^{(3)} \neq 0$ in the above algorithm. (Note that $\det(A_r) = a_{1,1} \, a_{2,2}^{(2)} \cdot \ldots \cdot a_{r,r}^{(r)}$; see the LU theorem (9.2).) If any of these numbers vanish, we can not continue the elimination in the stated form. For example, suppose the "pivot" $a_{1,1}$ were zero. Since $\det(A) \neq 0$, we know that $a_{i,1} \neq 0$ for some $i > 1$. If we interchange any such i-th row of A and b with the first row of A and b, we will obtain an equivalent equation system with $a_{1,1} \neq 0$. Then we can proceed with the algorithm stated in Sec. 9. An analogous cure would be possible at any stage where $a_{r,r}^{(r)} = 0$.

Unless a pivot is exactly zero, this interchange is unnecessary in theory. However, computing intuition suggests that if working with a zero pivot $a_{1,1}$ is impossible, then using a pivot $a_{1,1}$ which is close to zero will be inaccurate with arithmetic of limited precision. To verify this, consider the following example:

(10.1) **Example.** Assuming three-decimal floating arithmetic, we shall solve the system

(10.2)
$$\begin{cases} .000100x_1 + 1.00x_2 = 1.00 \\ 1.00 \quad\; x_1 + 1.00x_2 = 2.00. \end{cases}$$

The true solution, rounded to the decimals shown, is:

$$x_1 = \frac{10{,}000}{9999} = 1.00010; \qquad x_2 = \frac{9998}{9999} = 0.99990.$$

Here is the solution by Gaussian elimination without interchange:

$$\begin{cases} .000100x_1 + 1.00x_2 = 1.00 \\ \qquad\qquad -10{,}000x_2 = -10{,}000; \end{cases}$$
$$x_2 = 1.00;$$
$$x_1 = 0.00 \quad \text{(awful)}.$$

Here is the result by Gaussian elimination with interchange:

$$\begin{cases} 1.00x_1 + 1.00x_2 = 2.00 \\ \qquad\quad 1.00x_2 = 1.00; \end{cases}$$
$$x_2 = 1.00;$$
$$x_1 = 1.00 \quad \text{(perfect)}.$$

As such examples make clear, we must avoid pivots $a_{r,r}^{(r)}$ which are small in absolute value. A detailed round-off analysis in Sec. 21 shows that for general matrices it is advisable to keep the numbers $m_{i,j}$ less than or equal to one in absolute value. Therefore, one should choose as a pivot the largest in absolute value of the numbers $a_{i,r}^{(r)}$ ($i \geq r$) (or one of the largest if there are several). This is accomplished at each stage by interchanging rows r and i after determining that $a_{i,r}^{(r)}$ is an element of maximal absolute value in the column. This procedure is equivalent to interchanging the corresponding equations in the original system. If the multipliers $m_{i,j}$ are not being saved and if det (A) is not to be computed, then no record need be kept of the interchanges. However, if the multipliers are being saved for reuse later, there must be a record of which was the pivotal row at the elimination of the j-th column. And, of course, the sign of det (A) changes at each interchange.

We should note that in an automatic computer it is not necessary to interchange the rows of A and b. Instead, we may create an array of integers p_i ($i = 1, \ldots, n$) and call for $a_{p_i,j}$ instead of $a_{i,j}$. Thus the values of the permutation array p_i can replace the actual interchange. The method depends on the computing system involved.

Taking the pivot to be an element of largest absolute value in a column is called *partial pivoting strategy* by Wilkinson (1961). A more complicated elimination uses *complete pivoting strategy*, in which the pivot is taken to be an element of largest absolute value in the whole matrix of remaining equations. Although it is easier to prove certain things about the complete pivoting strategy, in practice the partial pivoting strategy appears to be entirely adequate; we will confine our attention to it.

There are some classes of matrices for which an entirely satisfactory round-off analysis can be given even if there is no search for pivots at all. The leading example is a positive definite, symmetric matrix A.

The detailed study in Sec. 21 shows that rounding errors are surprisingly small when the interchange strategy is followed. To put it roughly, in floating point the machine-computed solution x is actually the solution of a matrix problem $(A + \delta A)x = b$, where the elements of δA are not larger than approximately n individual round-off errors. We cannot say that x is so near to $A^{-1}b$. But, whenever the data A, b are subject to uncertainty, the uncertainty in x due to rounding error in the solution process is not more than approximately n times the uncertainty in x due merely to rounding the data when entering them into the machine!

An n-by-n *permutation matrix* is one in which every row and column contains exactly one 1 and $(n - 1)$ 0's. If P is a permutation matrix, then PA is A with its rows permuted and AP is A with its columns permuted.

By allowing row interchanges, we can drop the determinantal hypotheses of the LU theorem (9.2) and obtain the following:

(10.3) **Theorem.**   *If A is an arbitrary square matrix, there exist a permutation matrix P, a lower triangular matrix L with unit diagonal, and an upper triangular matrix U so that*

$$LU = PA.$$

However, L and U are not always uniquely determined by P and A.

A constructive proof is given by the algorithm *DECOMPOSE* in Sec. 16 and by Wendroff (1966).

II. SCALING EQUATIONS AND UNKNOWNS

In a system of linear equations $Ax = b$, frequently the unknowns x_j and the right members b_i have physical meanings. Perhaps the x_j's are displacements measured in centimeters and the b_i's are forces measured in dynes. Since such physical units are arbitrary, it is natural to ask: What if the displacement represented by one x_j had been measured in kilometers? In this special case, of course, we would make a substitution $x_j = 10^5 x_j'$. Then each term $a_{i,j} x_j$ would be replaced by $10^5 a_{i,j} x_j'$, and so the whole j-th column of A would be multiplied by 10^5.

Suppose, in general, that x_j is replaced by $d_j^{(2)} x_j'$, for $j = 1, \ldots, n$. Let D_2 be the nonsingular diagonal matrix

$$(11.1) \qquad D_2 = \begin{bmatrix} d_1^{(2)} & & \bigcirc \\ & \ddots & \\ \bigcirc & & d_n^{(2)} \end{bmatrix}.$$

The substitutions take the form

$$(11.2) \qquad x = D_2 x'.$$

Similarly, suppose that

$$(11.3) \qquad D_1 = \begin{bmatrix} d_1^{(1)} & & \bigcirc \\ & \ddots & \\ \bigcirc & & d_n^{(1)} \end{bmatrix}$$

is a second nonsingular matrix, and that we make the substitution

$$(11.4) \qquad b = D_1 b'$$

for the right member of the system $Ax = b$. Then the system becomes

$$A D_2 x' = D_1 b',$$

or

$$(11.5) \qquad D_1^{-1} A D_2 x' = b'.$$

Thus these simple changes of variable give us a new linear system whose matrix is $A' = D_1^{-1} A D_2$ and whose right-hand side is $b' = D_1^{-1} b$.

(11.6) **Definition.** A' is *diagonally equivalent to* A if nonsingular diagonal matrices D_1, D_2 exist so that

(11.7) $$A' = D_1^{-1}AD_2.$$

Thus $a'_{i,j} = [d_i^{(1)}]^{-1}a_{i,j}d_j^{(2)}$.

Clearly diagonal equivalence is an equivalence relation in the general mathematical sense (i.e., it is symmetric and transitive). It is also a special case of equivalence in the particular meaning used in matrix theory (because D_1 and D_2 are special nonsingular matrices).

We see that AD_2 is simply the matrix A with its columns multiplied by the factors $d_1^{(2)}, \ldots, d_n^{(2)}$. Moreover, $D_1^{-1}A$ is the matrix A with its rows multiplied by the factors $1/d_1^{(1)}, \ldots, 1/d_n^{(1)}$. The matrix $A' = D_1^{-1}AD_2$ is the result of performing both the column and the row multiplications on A. Because matrix multiplication is associative, it does not matter whether the row multiplications precede or follow the column multiplications. Moreover, because diagonal matrices commute under multiplication, it is possible to get from A to A' by performing the $2n$ multiplications of a row or column of A in any order.

It is common to speak of $D_1^{-1}AD_2$ as a *scaled equivalent* of A. In particular, AD_2 is a *column-scaled equivalent* of A, and $D_1^{-1}A$ is a *row-scaled equivalent* of A.

These scaling operations are commonly used in solving linear systems of equations. Although scaling can be important, it is not ordinarily necessary to choose the $d_i^{(1)}$'s and $d_j^{(2)}$'s with precision. In floating-point computation with base β, it is usually sufficient to choose the $d_i^{(1)}$'s and $d_i^{(2)}$'s to be integer powers of the base β. This changes only the exponents of the floating-point numbers $a_{i,j}$, leaving their *significands* (i.e., the fractional parts or mantissas) unchanged. Thus no rounding is introduced by such scaling.

(11.8) **Definition.** A' is *β-scaled equivalent to* A if $A' = D_1^{-1}AD_2$, where D_1, D_2 are nonsingular diagonal matrices whose diagonal elements are all integer powers of the floating-point base β.

Just as rows of A can be interchanged in practice without actually moving elements in the computer store, row and column scaling can be done without actually altering any $a_{i,j}$. It is necessary to store only the $2n$ numbers $d_i^{(1)}$ and $d_j^{(2)}$, or even only their exponents if they are all integer powers of β.

Naturally we want to know how scaling will affect the solution of a linear system. This subject is not very well understood, but we can state one firm result from Bauer (1963):

(11.9) **Theorem.**   *Let floating-point matrices A and A' be β-scaled equivalent in the sense of* (11.8). *Suppose that $b = D_1 b'$. Then, if the indices* *of the pivot elements and their order of selection have been fixed in advance, the solution by Gaussian elimination in floating-point arithmetic of the systems $Ax = b$ and $A'x' = b'$ will produce precisely the same significands in all answers and all intermediate numbers (unless there is an exponent overflow or underflow).*

The major assumption here is that the order of choosing pivots is predetermined and is the same for both systems. Naturally the solutions x and x' are related by (11.2).

Let us prove (11.9). We are assuming that round-off in the absence of exponent overflow or underflow is a property only of the significands and not of the exponents. The significands of A and A' are identical by the hypothesis. Because the order of pivoting is the same for both A and A', the arithmetic operations are performed at the same stage of the solution on corresponding elements of A, b and A', b'. Scaling a column of A just causes a compensating change in the exponent of the corresponding unknown. Scaling a row of $[A, b]$ just introduces a multiplying factor in one equation, and compensating changes of exponents occur in multipliers during the elimination. We shall not say more about column scaling, but we shall elaborate the effect of row scaling by considering one stage in the elimination of x_1. In this stage we have rows

$$a_i = [a_{i,1}, \ldots, a_{i,n}, b_i] \quad \text{and} \quad a_k = [a_{k,1}, \ldots, a_{k,n}, b_k].$$

Assume that $a_{i,1}$ is the pivot element for the first column. In the elimination of x_1 from the k-th row, we replace a_k by

$$a_k^{(2)} = a_k - \frac{a_{k,1}}{a_{i,1}} \cdot a_i.$$

Now suppose that the matrix $[A', b']$ has been obtained by scaling a_i with β^r and a_k with β^s. Then, in solving $A'x' = b'$, we form the new row

$$\beta^s a_k - \frac{\beta^s a_{k,1}}{\beta^r a_{i,1}} \cdot \beta^r a_i,$$

which is precisely $\beta^s a_k^{(2)}$. Hence the row scaling only multiplies the new row $a_k^{(2)}$ by β^s; the β^r factor does not appear. Such scaling can have no essential effect on the subsequent elimination or back solution. This concludes our proof of (11.9).

We conclude from theorem (11.9) that the only possible effect that scaling a matrix by integer powers of β can have on elimination is to alter the choice of pivot elements. We shall now give two examples to show that scaling can indeed make a large difference. In both examples we take $\beta = 10$ and use three-decimal floating-point arithmetic and partial pivoting.

(11.10) **Example.** We take the example of (10.1) and multiply the first equation by 10^5:

$$\begin{cases} 10.0x_1 + 100,000x_2 = 100,000 \\ 1.00x_1 + \quad\; 1.00x_2 = 2.00. \end{cases}$$

Because $10.0 > 1.00$, the partial pivoting strategy calls for no interchange of the equations. Thus the elimination yields

$$\begin{cases} 10.0x_1 + 100,000x_2 = 100,000 \\ \qquad\quad -10,000x_2 = -10,000. \end{cases}$$

Solving,
$$\begin{cases} x_2 = 1.00 \\ x_1 = 0.00 \quad \text{(awful!).} \end{cases}$$

Thus scaling the first row forced selecting the pivot element from the first equation. The elimination proceeded just as it did in (10.1) without the interchange strategy, which we saw to be so important for this example. The example itself is also an illustration of theorem (11.9), as the reader will see if he compares it with the first solution of (10.1).

Since column scaling by itself has no effect on the choice of pivots in the first column, example (11.10) could be rewritten in the two following ways without essential change in the result:

$$\begin{cases} 10.0x_1 + \qquad 1.00x_2 = 1.00_{10}5 \\ 1.00x_1 + 1.00_{10}-5x_2 = 2.00 \end{cases}$$

or
$$\begin{cases} 1.00x_1 + \qquad 1.00x_2 = 1.00_{10}5 \\ .100x_1 + 1.00_{10}-5x_2 = 2.00. \end{cases}$$

(In these and later examples we use the ALGOL 60 notation of expressing numbers with base 10. Thus $1.00_{10}-5$ is 1.00×10^{-5}.)

In spite of the very poor first solution obtained in example (11.10), iterative improvement (discussed in Sec. 13) does result in a correct answer.

The second example is of order 3.

(11.11) **Example.** Consider the system

(11.12)
$$\left\{ \begin{array}{r} x_1 + 2x_2 + 3x_3 = 6 \\ x_1 - x_2 + x_3 = 1 \\ 2_{10}{-}4x_1 + x_2 + x_3 = 2. \end{array} \right.$$

Correctly rounded, the solution is

$$(1.0010, \quad 1.0004, \quad .9994).$$

Solving the system by Gaussian elimination with partial pivoting and working in three-decimal floating-point arithmetic, we get after the forward elimination

(11.13)
$$\left\{ \begin{array}{r} x_1 + 2x_2 + 3x_3 = 6 \\ -3x_2 - 2x_3 = -5 \\ .332x_3 = .333. \end{array} \right.$$

Back solving, we get

$$x^{(0)} = (1.00, \quad 1.00, \quad 1.00).$$

Substituting into (11.12), we get the residual $b - Ax^{(0)} = \theta$. Thus the correctly rounded, three-decimal solution is obtained easily.

Let A be the matrix of (11.12):

(11.14)
$$A = \begin{bmatrix} 1 & 2 & 3 \\ 1 & -1 & 1 \\ 2_{10}{-}4 & 1 & 1 \end{bmatrix} ; \quad \text{let } b = \begin{bmatrix} 6 \\ 1 \\ 2 \end{bmatrix} .$$

An extensive computation shows that cond $(A) = 27.4$, quite a low number. Let

(11.15)
$$D_1^{-1} = \begin{bmatrix} 1 & & \\ & 1 & \\ & & {}_{10}4 \end{bmatrix} ; \quad D_2 = \begin{bmatrix} 1 & & \\ & {}_{10}{-}4 & \\ & & {}_{10}{-}4 \end{bmatrix} .$$

Scaling with (11.7) and (11.15), the system (11.12) becomes

$$(11.16) \qquad \begin{cases} x_1 + 2_{10}{-}4x_2 + 3_{10}{-}4x_3 = 6 \\ x_1 - {}_{10}{-}4x_2 + {}_{10}{-}4x_3 = 1 \\ 2x_1 + \quad x_2 + \qquad x_3 = 2_{10}4. \end{cases}$$

Solving by either a partial or complete pivotal strategy, we choose 2 as our first pivot and eliminate x_1 to obtain

$$\begin{cases} 2x_1 + \quad x_2 + \quad x_3 = 2_{10}4 \\ -.500x_2 - .500x_3 = -_{10}4 \\ -.500x_2 - .500x_3 = -_{10}4. \end{cases}$$

Elimination of x_2 leads to the system

$$(11.17) \qquad \begin{cases} 2x_1 + \quad x_2 + \quad x_3 = 2_{10}4 \\ -.500x_2 - .500x_3 = -_{10}4 \\ 0 = 0, \end{cases}$$

which is singular.

Thus, in this example, scaling makes the normal pivoting strategies inadequate. By Bauer's theorem (11.9), it would be satisfactory to solve (11.16) with $a_{1,1}$ as first pivot, for this would be equivalent to what was done in deriving (11.13). Because (11.17) is a singular system, we see no way to solve (11.16) from (11.17) by iterative improvement (described in Sec. 13). In this sense (11.11) is a worse example than (11.10), proving that the need for proper scaling of a matrix is very compelling if we are to devise a program to solve as many linear equation systems as possible.

In our discussion (Sec. 8) of the effect of perturbing A and b on the solution of a linear system, the critical parameter was cond (A). In our proof (Sec. 22) of the convergence of the iterative-improvement method for solving linear systems, the essential hypothesis is that the same number cond (A) be small enough. It is therefore generally agreed that theoretically the best way to scale a matrix is to make the condition number of the transformed matrix as small as possible. We may then pose the problems:

(11.18) Given a matrix A, what choice of diagonal matrices D_1 and D_2 will cause cond $(D_1^{-1}AD_2)$ to be a minimum?

(11.19)   Given a matrix A, can we determine the minimizing D_1 and D_2 of
(11.18) or reasonably good approximations of them with a sufficiently
fast computer algorithm?

Problem (11.18) turns out to be completely solved for certain matrix
norms. (Recall that cond $(A) = \|A\| \cdot \|A^{-1}\|$, so that the solution depends on
the choice of norm.) It has not been solved for the euclidean norm, which
we are mainly using in this book, except for two special cases: (i) when
$n = 2$ for any A; (ii) when both A and A^{-1} have certain distributions of signs
called *checkerboard patterns* (see Bauer (1963) for the meaning of this term).
When the minimizing D_1 and D_2 are known, they depend in an essential way
on the matrix A^{-1}. Since our object in scaling A is to help determine $A^{-1}b$,
we certainly do not know A^{-1}. Hence we cannot expect to use the known
solution of (11.18) to solve the problem (11.19).

We shall now state the solution of Bauer (1963) to problem (11.18) for
the maximum norm. Recall that when $\|x\|_\infty$ is defined by (2.15), the corre-
sponding matrix norm $\|A\|_\infty$ is

(11.20) $$\|A\|_\infty = \max_{1 \leq i \leq n} \sum_{j=1}^{n} |a_{i,j}|.$$

For any matrix $B = (b_{i,j})$, define $|B|$ to be the matrix of nonnegative elements
$|b_{i,j}|$.

Let A be a given irreducible matrix; see (6.4). Let $C = |A| \cdot |A^{-1}|$. Since
C has nonnegative elements, it is known (Varga (1962)) that one of its eigenvalues of maximum modulus is simple, real, and positive; we call it ρ.
The matrix also has a column eigenvector $u = (u_1, \ldots, u_n)^T$ corresponding
to ρ so that $Cu = \rho u$. For $i = 1, \ldots, n$, let $d_i^{(1)} = u_i$. The matrix D_1 is
given by (11.3) in terms of these $d_i^{(1)}$. Similarly, the matrix $|A^{-1}| \cdot |A|$ has ρ
as a unique positive eigenvalue of maximum modulus and has a corre-
sponding column eigenvector $v = (v_1, \ldots, v_n)^T$. For $j = 1, \ldots, n$, let
$d_j^{(2)} = v_j$. The matrix D_2 is given by (11.1) in terms of these $d_j^{(2)}$. The D_1
and D_2 just computed minimize cond $(D_1^{-1}AD_2)$. (Since cond (B) is unaffected
by multiplying B by a scalar, the scaling of the vectors u and v is irrelevant
to the problem. That is, D_1 and D_2 are unique only up to multiplicative
constants.) This concludes Bauer's solution to problem (11.18) for the norm
$\|x\|_\infty$.

The solution for the euclidean norm $\|x\|$ (for special matrices A) also
involves the matrices $|A| \cdot |A^{-1}|$ and $|A^{-1}| \cdot |A|$ and their eigenvectors, but it
is somewhat more complicated. A good scaling in terms of the norm $\|x\|_\infty$
should always be satisfactory in terms of $\|x\|$ because it can be shown that,
for matrices of order n,

(11.21) $$\frac{1}{n} \leq \frac{\text{cond}_\infty (A)}{\text{cond} (A)} \leq n.$$

Here cond $(A) = \|A\| \cdot \|A^{-1}\|$ with respect to $\|x\|$, while $\text{cond}_\infty (A) = \|A\|_\infty \cdot \|A^{-1}\|_\infty$. But, in any case, we know of no satisfactory practical solution to the scaling problem (11.19) which will work for all matrices A in any norm.

(11.22) **Exercise.** Prove (11.21).

As a matter of curiosity, our colleague James Varah made an experimental determination of D_1 and D_2 so that cond $(D_1^{-1}AD_2)$ is minimized in the euclidean norm, for the matrix A of (11.14). He found that

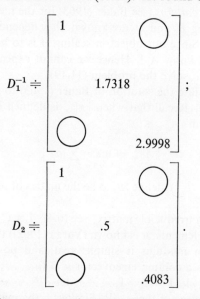

$$D_1^{-1} \doteq \begin{bmatrix} 1 & & \bigcirc \\ & 1.7318 & \\ \bigcirc & & 2.9998 \end{bmatrix};$$

$$D_2 \doteq \begin{bmatrix} 1 & & \bigcirc \\ & .5 & \\ \bigcirc & & .4083 \end{bmatrix}.$$

The minimum value was cond $(D_1^{-1}AD_2) \doteq 13.9427$, compared with cond $(A) \doteq 27.4$.

The approach to the scaling problem taken by Wilkinson (1961) is to insist that a matrix A be *equilibrated* before a linear-system solver is applied. Roughly, a matrix is equilibrated if all its rows and columns have approximately the same length in some norm. The round-off analysis given in Sec. 21 for Gaussian elimination gives the most effective results when a matrix is equilibrated because then a small perturbation of one row (or column) of the matrix is of the same magnitude as that of any other row (or column) of the matrix.

(11.23) **Definition.** A matrix A is *row equilibrated* (relative to the norm $\|x\|_\infty$) if for each row index i

$$\beta^{-1} \leq \max_{1 \leq j \leq n} |a_{i,j}| \leq 1,$$

where β is the number base of the floating-point system.

(11.24) **Definition.** A matrix A is *column equilibrated* (relative to the norm $\|x\|_\infty$) if for each column index j

$$\beta^{-1} \le \max_{1 \le i \le n} |a_{i,j}| \le 1.$$

(11.25) **Definition.** A matrix A is *equilibrated* if it is both row equilibrated and column equilibrated.

The use of β permits a matrix to be equilibrated by changes of exponent only.

Wilkinson's advice is that one approximately equilibrate the coefficient matrix before solving a system of equations. Unfortunately there is no unique equilibrated form of a matrix. Various equilibration algorithms will change it into very different equilibrated matrices. For example, let $\beta = 10$ and let

$$A = \begin{pmatrix} 1 & 1 & 2_{10}9 \\ 2 & -1 & {}_{10}9 \\ 1 & 2 & 0 \end{pmatrix}.$$

If we first equilibrate the columns of A, we get

$$B = \begin{pmatrix} .1 & .1 & .2 \\ .2 & -.1 & .1 \\ .1 & .2 & 0 \end{pmatrix},$$

which is also row equilibrated. But, if we first equilibrate the rows of A, we get

$$C = \begin{pmatrix} {}_{10}{-}10 & {}_{10}{-}10 & .2 \\ 2_{10}{-}10 & -{}_{10}{-}10 & .1 \\ .1 & .2 & 0 \end{pmatrix},$$

which is also column equilibrated. Certainly B and C differ markedly in their condition and scaling and in the choice of pivots for a Gaussian elimination.* B is a much more satisfactory scaling of the matrix A.

Although one can undoubtedly always find a reasonable scaling of a matrix of order 3 by inspection, it is quite unclear to us how to program a reasonable scaling of a general matrix. The algorithms known to us, like that of McKeeman (1962), do not furnish a universal solution to the problem.

* We thank R. W. Hamming for calling our attention to this type of example.

In the algorithms of this book for solving linear equation systems, we have used only a scaling by rows. That is, we have found a matrix D_1 so that the matrix $D_1 A$ has each of its rows of equal length in the sense of the maximum norm $\| \ \|_\infty$. We do not claim this to be an optimal solution to the scaling problem, which, as we have tried to show, is more complicated. In our codes the row scaling is actually done implicitly by storing the appropriate scaling coefficients rather than explicitly by altering the matrix elements (see Sec. 16).

12. THE CROUT AND DOOLITTLE VARIANTS

Crout's method without interchanges, designed expressly for desk calculators, eliminates the writing of the intermediate numbers like $a_{4,4}^{(2)}$ in Sec. 9. Instead, the numbers $m_{i,j}$ and $u_{i,j}$ are computed one-by-one by a continuous accumulation of products. (Actually this is Doolittle's method. The now better-known name of Crout is properly associated with a decomposition $A = LU$ in which the $u_{i,i} = 1$ and the diagonal elements of L are (ordinarily) different from 1. The distinction is minor.)

Let $b_i = a_{i,5}$ $(i = 1, \ldots, 4)$. The Crout algorithm for a system of order 4 is this:

for $j := 1, 2, 3, 4, 5$ **do** $u_{1,j} := a_{1,j}$;

for $i := 2, 3, 4$ **do** $m_{i,1} := a_{i,1}/u_{1,1}$;

for $j := 2, 3, 4, 5$ **do** $u_{2,j} := a_{2,j} - m_{2,1} \times u_{1,j}$;

for $i := 3, 4$ **do** $m_{i,2} := (a_{i,2} - m_{i,1} \times u_{1,2})/u_{2,2}$;

for $j := 3, 4, 5$ **do** $u_{3,j} := a_{3,j} - m_{3,1} \times u_{1,j} - m_{3,2} \times u_{2,j}$;

$m_{4,3} := (a_{4,3} - m_{4,1} \times u_{1,3} - m_{4,2} \times u_{2,3})/u_{3,3}$;

for $j = 4, 5$ **do** $u_{4,j} := a_{4,j} - m_{4,1} \times u_{1,j} - m_{4,2} \times u_{2,j} - m_{4,3} \times u_{3,j}$.

We get the numbers $u_{i,j}$ and $m_{i,j}$ of Gaussian elimination precisely, without any intermediate writing. Note that Crout's method is essentially a constructive computation of L, U in the LU theorem, in a slightly different order from that given in our inductive proof of (9.2). The amount of arithmetic is the same in the Crout method as in Gaussian elimination since the same operations are carried out, although in a different order.

For symmetric matrices A, one can reduce the arithmetic by half by computing G in the decomposition $A = GG^T$; see (9.3). The interchanges will upset the symmetry unless one interchanges columns and rows together. If the matrix is symmetric and also positive definite, Wilkinson (1961) has proved that interchanges may be omitted without serious increase in round-off error, and this omission simplifies the programming for this quite frequently occurring matrix.

Is the Crout method preferable to Gaussian elimination? On a desk calculator it is a great gain to avoid the intermediate recordings, but this is less important with an automatic computer. The interchanges are difficult to manage with pencil and paper using Crout and easier using Gaussian elimination. However, there is no difficulty with the interchanges in using Crout with an automatic computer. The Crout algorithm has the smaller round-off error, providing the machine (like the IBM 7090) can easily store an accumulating product in a double-length register and round it off to single precision only when the final number is stored. If the machine, like the Burroughs B5500, cannot do this easily, then using Crout has no advantage.

13. ITERATIVE IMPROVEMENT

Even though the round-off error in elimination with interchanges for a well-scaled matrix is quite low, sometimes one would like to achieve more accuracy. For example, in changing coordinates by a similarity transformation in the computation of eigenvalues, one needs to know that S^{-1} is as accurate an inverse of a matrix S as can be computed in single-precision. In other cases, a demanding customer may insist on having $A^{-1}b$ to great accuracy, even though the data do not warrant it! It is therefore interesting that high-accuracy solutions x can be obtained to most linear systems $Ax = b$ and that it can be done with only a modest (about 25 per cent) increase in time over obtaining the first solution x.

In this section we shall use the notations x_1, x_2, r_1, etc. to denote vectors rather than components of vectors.

The key to improving the accuracy of a first solution x_1 is a double-precision computation of its *residual* $r_1 = b - Ax_1$. Knowing r_1, we then solve the system

$$Az_1 = r_1.$$

If we knew z_1 precisely, then $x_2 = x_1 + z_1$ would solve the system $Ax = b$ precisely because

$$Ax_2 = A(x_1 + z_1) = Ax_1 + Az_1 = Ax_1 + r_1 = b.$$

If we know z_1 to a few digits, these digits usually furnish an x_2 which is more accurate than x_1. Forming $r_2 = b - Ax_2$, we can then compute z_2 and x_3. The single-precision vectors $x_1, x_2, \ldots$ typically form a sequence which quickly becomes constant at a vector which as a solution of $Ax = b$ is accurate to full single precision. Note that each system $Az_k = r_k$ has the same matrix A, and so we can make use of the multipliers $m_{i,j}$ already stored from the first solution. (See Sec. 9.) This is why iterative improvement of a first solution adds only a moderate amount to the computational time of the algorithm.

It is absolutely essential that the residuals r_k be computed with a higher precision than that of the rest of the computation. This is a general principle in all equation solving: Calculation of the residual is the critical computation and must be done with the most accuracy. It is rarely necessary to achieve such high accuracy in any other part of the algorithm. As another example of this principle, in using Newton's process to compute an isolated zero of a real-valued function $f(x)$, one may ordinarily be rather inaccurate in computing the derivative $f'(x_i)$ but the residual $f(x_i)$ must be accurate.

49

Note that the error e_1 in x_1 has a simple relation to r_1:

$$e_1 = x_1 - A^{-1}b = A^{-1}(Ax_1 - b) = -A^{-1}r_1.$$

Thus

(13.1)
$$\|e_1\| \leq \|A^{-1}\| \cdot \|r_1\|.$$

A detailed round-off analysis of Gaussian elimination is given in Sec. 21, and a proof of the convergence of iterative improvement, in Sec. 22. The following discussion is intended to give the reader some plausible insight into the nature of the algorithm. In particular, we wish to show that the value of cond (A) determines roughly how rapidly the sequence x_k converges to its final value. Conversely, the convergence of x_k can be used to furnish a rough estimate of cond (A).

Suppose for definiteness, that we work on a t-digit, base-β, floating-point computing system (see Sec. 20). Thus a unit round-off error in any number y is approximately $\beta^{-t}|y|$. To introduce notation for the components of x_1 and r_1, we let

$$x_1 = (x_1^{(1)}, x_2^{(1)}, \ldots, x_n^{(1)})$$

and
$$r_1 = (r_1^{(1)}, r_2^{(1)}, \ldots, r_n^{(1)}).$$

Since $r_1 = b - Ax_1$, we have

(13.2)
$$r_i^{(1)} = b_i - a_{i,1}x_1^{(1)} - a_{i,2}x_2^{(1)} - \cdots - a_{i,n}x_n^{(1)}.$$

Now Gaussian elimination determines the single-precision components $x_j^{(1)}$ of x_1 so that the components $r_i^{(1)}$ of r_1 in (13.2) are roughly as small as possible. Most of the digits of the terms $a_{i,j}x_j^{(1)}$ in the i-th sum (13.2) cancel with each other and with some leading digits of b_i. This leaves an i-th component $r_i^{(1)}$ that is roughly the size of the least significant digits of the largest (in absolute value) of the terms $a_{i,j}x_j^{(1)}$—that is, $\beta^{-t} \max_j |a_{i,j}| \cdot |x_j^{(1)}|$. Hence, roughly speaking,

$$\|r_1\| \doteq \beta^{-t}\|A\| \cdot \|x_1\|.$$

Since (13.1) is normally approximately an equality, it follows that

$$\|e_1\| \doteq \|A^{-1}\| \cdot \|A\| \cdot \|x_1\|\beta^{-t} = \text{cond } (A) \, \|x_1\|\beta^{-t}.$$

Hence, if cond $(A) \doteq \beta^p$,

$$\|e_1\| \doteq \|x_1\|\beta^{p-t}.$$

If $p > t$, then the error $\|e_1\|$ will be larger than $\|x_1\|$, and we will have gained

much more slowly at first than the error e_k:

$$\|r_1\| = .0000\ 34;$$

$$\|r_2\| = .0000\ 015;$$

$$\|r_3\| = .0000\ 095.$$

Even though $\|e_3\| \doteq \tfrac{1}{10}\|e_2\|$, we have $\|r_3\| \doteq 6\|r_2\|$ (!). This behavior is typical of ill-conditioned systems. It is essentially due to the fact that r_2 is about as small as a five-figure x can give. Even r_1 is less than half a unit in the last digits of b. Thus the main behavior of the iteration is that $\|r_k\|$ remains reasonably constant while $\|e_k\|$ drops from a relatively large $\|e_1\|$ down to full single-precision accuracy.

Finally, we should note that x_1 is already as accurate an answer as the data warrant. If the right-hand side were changed by half a unit in the last place to $b^* = (2.49445, 2.39885)$, then the true solution would be close to

$$x^* = A^{-1}b^* = (1.318605, 1.147017).$$

In the neighborhood of the solution $A^{-1}b$ the set of floating-decimal vectors ($\beta = 10$, $t = 5$) form a square lattice L in the x plane, with mesh width 10^{-4}. Clearly the closest lattice point x to $A^{-1}b$ is found by rounding $A^{-1}b$ to the fourth decimal place. The transformation A maps this square lattice into a lattice AL of parallelograms in the range space. Since cond $(A) \doteq 4000$, the parallelograms could be as much as approximately 4000 times as long as they are wide. Thus the lattice point x closest to $A^{-1}b$ seems likely to be mapped into a lattice point Ax that is farther from b than other points of AL. Indeed, our computations show that this did happen. Thus the minima of $\|Ax - b\|$ and of $\|x - A^{-1}b\|$ do not occur for the same x. Although given here in terms of a particular example, this phenomenon is a general one for linear systems.

(13.3) **Exercise.**   Use a computer search (or analysis if possible) to find that vector x out of the class of floating-decimal vectors with five significant decimals ($\beta = 10$, $t = 5$) which minimizes $\|r\|_2 = \|b - Ax\|_2$. Is the answer x_3?

(13.4) **Exercise.**   Let x_1 be an approximate solution of the linear system $Ax = b$, where $b \neq \theta$. Let $e_1 = x_1 - A^{-1}b$ and $r_1 = b - Ax_1$. Define the *relative error* of x_1 by

$$\rho_x = \|e_1\|/\|A^{-1}b\|$$

and the corresponding *relative residual* by

$$\rho_r = \|r_1\|/\|b\|.$$

Prove that

(13.5)
$$\frac{1}{\text{cond}\,(A)} \leq \frac{\rho_x}{\rho_r} \leq \text{cond}\,(A),$$

and, moreover, that for any A, in exact arithmetic, either inequality in (13.5) can be made an equality by appropriate choices of b and x_1.

14. COMPUTING THE DETERMINANT

Recall from our proof of the LU theorem (9.2) that

(14.1) $$\det (A) = u_{1,1} \cdot u_{2,2} \cdot \ldots \cdot u_{n,n}.$$

The determinant of A is desired frequently enough that a complete linear equation solver should provide it. There is one perhaps unexpected programming problem in multiplying the $u_{i,i}$ together, namely the probability of exponent overflow or underflow. For $n \geq 20$, for example, the magnitude of a determinant can be very large or very small even though the matrix elements are of magnitude 1. This necessitates a special product subroutine which permits exponents far beyond those encountered in usual floating-point arithmetic. At Stanford University in various routines we have used a special two-variable version of the developing product. One variable is a floating-point number whose absolute value is relatively close to one—for example, in the range $[10^{-10}, 10^{10}]$ or even $[10^{-1}, 1]$. The second integer variable is an exponent associated with the product. Before each multiplication a check for possible overflow or underflow is made and the exponents are adjusted if necessary. The final product is converted to a normal single-word floating-point number when possible. If any factor is zero, an early exit can be made, of course.

Another solution to the magnitude problem is to compute

(14.2) $$\log |\det (A)| = \sum_{i=1}^{n} \log |u_{i,i}|$$

and make special provision for the sign and case of zero $u_{i,i}$. However, this use of logarithms may result in some loss of accuracy because of cancellation in the sum (14.2), whereas an extended product can be computed with very little round-off error, as the reader of Sec. 20 can show. The loss of accuracy can be prevented by double-precision accumulation of the sum (14.2). If a double-precision logarithm function is available, it is worthwhile to use it, but double-precision accumulation of the sum (14.2) is probably useful even when the logarithms are correct only to single precision.

As has been pointed out by Kahan (1965a), a good floating-point computing system should be capable of counting exponent overflows and underflows as they occur and of informing the main program of these without interruption and without loss of leading digits. Such a system would obviate the necessity of making special provisions for computing determinants. Unfortunately, it does not appear likely that such systems will be widely available in the near future.

15. NEARLY SINGULAR MATRICES

In the linear equation system $Ax = b$, if the matrix A is actually singular, we lose the mathematical basis for ordinary methods of solving the system. Such a system has a solution only for certain right-hand sides b, and, whenever a solution exists, others can be found by adding to one solution any solution u of the homogeneous system $Au = \theta$.

We are not sure what a computer program should do with a singular matrix A. For the moment, let us ignore matters of round-off and assume a purely mathematical problem.

If the matrix A is considered a collection of column vectors $c_1, \ldots, c_n$, where c_j is the j-th column of A, solving the linear system $Ax = b$ can be interpreted as a search for n real numbers $x_1, \ldots, x_n$ so that

$$(15.1) \qquad b = x_1 c_1 + \cdots + x_n c_n.$$

If the matrix A is singular, the columns c_j are linearly dependent. From this viewpoint, perhaps a program should find the rank r of the set of columns. Then perhaps it should find a subset of r of the n columns which in some sense form as "well conditioned" a basis as possible for the column space. Finally, perhaps it should state whether or not b is in this column space, and, if it is, find the representation of b as a linear combination of the r basis vectors:

$$b = x_1 c_1 + \cdots + x_r c_r,$$

where we have assumed for notational convenience that the first r columns form the basis. The program might also express each column c_j not in the basis as a linear combination of basis columns.

On the other hand, the matrix A can be thought of as a collection of row vectors $r_1, \ldots, r_n$, where r_i is the i-th row of A. Then we can interpret solving the system $Ax = b$ as the search for a column vector x so that

$$(15.2) \qquad r_1 x = b_1, \ldots, r_n x = b_n.$$

If the matrix A is singular, the rows $r_1, \ldots, r_n$ are linearly dependent. From the row viewpoint, perhaps a program should find the rank r of the matrix, and a subset of r rows which form a "well-conditioned" row basis. Then perhaps it should state whether a vector x exists so that (15.2) is true, and, if so, produce it. The program might also express each other row of A as a linear combination of the rows of the basis.

The reason that we used "perhaps" so much in the above discussion is that there does not seem to be an agreed-upon set of actions for a singular matrix. We do not know what customers of linear equation solvers really want. Moreover, it is not clear that there is any way of determining a reasonable rank of the given matrix as a by-product of the forward elimination. Greatly complicating the situation is the fact that the sharp mathematical distinction between singular and nonsingular matrices exists only in the mathematician's ideal world of real numbers. As soon as we operate upon matrices with rounded arithmetic the distinction necessarily becomes fuzzy. Thus certain nonsingular matrices may be made singular as a result of the perturbations introduced by round-off. More likely, a truly singular input matrix will be perturbed into a neighboring nonsingular matrix by the round-off. This means that in computing practice there are probably a considerable number of nearly singular matrices which will require special treatment in any complete linear equation solver.

In our linear equation solving algorithms of Secs. 16 and 17 the presence of a singular or nearly singular matrix A will be revealed in one of two ways:

(15.1)　　at some stage in the elimination all elements of the pivotal column turn out to be exactly zero;

or

(15.2)　　the iterative improvement built into our algorithm fails to converge.

Condition (15.1) is unlikely to occur unless the singularity of A is a particularly simple one since normally round-off modifies some element of the pivotal column to a nonzero value. Condition (15.2) can and does occur for some matrices, and we should have some definite suggestion as to what to do next. The present codes merely provide an exit to an error procedure *SINGULAR* and assume that the user of the programs will provide his own recovery routine if he knows what he wants to do.

An important project is to develop a good program which will recover gracefully from either of the above indications of near singularity. In our opinion, such a program might use a complete pivotal strategy to locate a sufficiently well-conditioned r-by-r minor M of A, in which r would be the approximate rank of A. The rows in M would form the row basis of A, and the columns, the column basis of A. We hesitate to predict any further how the program might go. Possibly some aspects of a least-squares solution of inconsistent equations would be used, including some aspects of the problem of computing the pseudoinverse of A. See Golub (1965), Businger and Golub (1965), and Golub and Kahan (1965).

For a discussion of singularity and near singularity in other contexts of numerical analysis, see Forsythe (1958), where it is argued that nearly singular problems cause more computing difficulty than truly singular ones and that nearly singular problems are best treated by methods which in some sense are close to methods for singular problems.

16. ALGOL 60 PROGRAM

Computer programs that use Gaussian elimination or one of its variants have been written in many programming languages and used on many computers. Several of these programs have also used some form of iterative improvement. Together with William McKeeman we have developed the set of four ALGOL 60 procedures now to be given as program (16.1). Earlier versions of this program are found in Forsythe (1960) and McKeeman (1962). See Baumann *et al.* (1964) and Naur *et al.* (1963) for an introduction to and a definition of the ALGOL 60 language. Several pages of explanation follow our program.

(16.1)   ALGOL 60 program for solving linear systems

```
begin
   comment Linear system package, ALGOL 60 version;
   integer array ps[1:100]; comment Global pivot index array. We
                            assume n ≤ 100;
   procedure DECOMPOSE(n, A, LU);
   value n; integer n;
   real array A, LU; comment A, LU[1:n, 1:n];
   comment Uses global integer array ps;
   comment Computes triangular matrices L and U and per-
           mutation matrix P so that LU = PA. Stores L − I
           and U in LU. Array ps contains permuted row
           indices;
   comment DECOMPOSE(n, A, A) overwrites A with LU;
begin
   real array scales[1:n];
   integer i, j, k, pivotindex;
   real normrow, pivot, size, biggest, mult;
   comment Initialize ps, LU and scales;
   for i := 1 step 1 until n do
      begin
      ps[i] := i;
      normrow := 0;
      for j := 1 step 1 until n do
      begin
         LU[i,j] := A[i,j];
         if normrow < abs(LU[i,j]) then normrow := abs(LU[i,j]);
      end;
```

```
      if normrow ≠ 0 then scales[i] := 1/normrow
          else begin scales[i] := 0; SINGULAR(0) end;
  end;
  comment Gaussian elimination with partial pivoting;
  for k := 1 step 1 until n − 1 do
  begin
      biggest := 0;
      for i := k step 1 until n do
      begin
          size := abs(LU[ps[i], k]) × scales[ps[i]];
          if biggest < size then
              begin biggest := size; pivotindex := i end;
      end;
      if biggest = 0 then
          begin SINGULAR(1); go to endkloop end;
      if pivotindex ≠ k then
          begin
              j := ps[k]; ps[k] := ps[pivotindex]; ps[pivotindex] := j
          end;
      pivot := LU[ps[k], k];
      for i := k + 1 step 1 until n do
      begin
          LU[ps[i], k] := mult := LU[ps[i], k]/pivot;
          if mult ≠ 0 then
          for j := k + 1 step 1 until n do
              LU[ps[i], j] := LU[ps[i], j] − mult × LU[ps[k], j];
              comment Inner loop. Only column subscript varies. Use
                      machine code if necessary for efficiency;
      end;
  endkloop:
  end;
  if LU[ps[n], n] = 0 then SINGULAR(1);
end DECOMPOSE;
```

```
procedure SOLVE(n, LU, b, x);
    value n; integer n;
    real array LU, b, x; comment LU[1:n, 1:n], b, x[1:n];
    comment Uses global integer array ps;
    comment Solves Ax = b using LU from DECOMPOSE;
begin
    integer i, j;
    real dot;
```

```
for i := 1 step 1 until n do
begin
  dot := 0;
  for j := 1 step 1 until i − 1 do
    dot := dot + LU[ps[i],j] × x[j];
  x[i] := b[ps[i]] − dot;
end;
for i := n step − 1 until 1 do
begin
  dot := 0;
  for j := i + 1 step 1 until n do
    dot := dot + LU[ps[i],j] × x[j];
  x[i] := (x[i] − dot)/LU[ps[i], i];
end;
comment As in DECOMPOSE, the inner loops involve only the
        column subscript of LU and may be machine coded
        for efficiency;
end SOLVE;
```

```
procedure IMPROVE(n, A, LU, b, x, digits);
  value n; integer n;
  real array A, LU, b, x; comment A, LU[1:n, 1:n], b, x[1:n];
  real digits;
  comment A is the original matrix, LU is from DECOMPOSE, b
          is the right-hand side, x is solution from SOLVE.
          Improves x to machine accuracy and sets digits to the
          number of digits of x which do not change;
  comment Machine-dependent quantities indicated by 0-0;
begin
  real array r, dx[1:n];
  integer iter, itmax, i;
  real t, normx, normdx, eps;
  real procedure log(x); value x; real x;
    log := .4342944819 × ln(x);
  real procedure accumdotprod(n, A, i, x, extraterm);
    value n, i, extraterm; integer n, i; real extraterm;
    real array A, x;
    comment This procedure should evaluate the inner product of
            the i-th row of the array A with the vector x, then
            add extraterm to the result. The multiplication
            A[i,j] × x[j] must yield a double-precision result and
            all the additions must be done in double precision.
```

The body of the procedure cannot be written in
ALGOL 60;

comment The body of *accumdotprod* could be written as
follows in terms of the code procedure *innerprod* on
p. 206 of Martin, Peters, and Wilkinson (1966):

begin
    real $d1, d2$
    integer k
    $innerprod(1, 1, n, extraterm, 0, A[i, k], x[k], k, d1, d2)$
    $accumdotprod := d1$
end;
begin
    comment $\langle$code$\rangle$;
    $accumdotprod := 0\text{-}0$; **comment** 0-0 indicates code result;
end *accumdotprod;*
$eps := 0\text{-}0$; **comment** Machine-dependent round-off level;
$itmax := 0\text{-}0$; **comment** Use approximately $2 \times \log(1/eps)$;
$normx := 0$;
for $i := 1$ **step** 1 **until** n **do**
    if $normx < abs(x[i])$ **then** $normx := abs(x[i])$;
if $normx = 0$ **then**
    begin $digits := -log(eps)$; **go to** *converged* **end;**
for $iter := 1$ **step** 1 **until** $itmax$ **do**
begin
    for $i := 1$ **step** 1 **until** n **do**
        $r[i] := -accumdotprod(n, A, i, x, -b[i])$;
    $SOLVE(n, LU, r, dx)$;
    $normdx := 0$;
    for $i := 1$ **step** 1 **until** n **do**
    begin
        $t := x[i]$;
        $x[i] := x[i] + dx[i]$;
        if $normdx < abs(x[i] - t)$ **then** $normdx := abs(x[i] - t)$;
    end;
    if $iter = 1$ **then**
        $digits := -log($**if** $normdx \neq 0$ **then** $normdx/normx$
                        else $eps)$;
    if $normdx \leq eps \times normx$ **then go to** *converged;*
end *iter;*
comment Iteration did not converge;
$SINGULAR(2)$;
converged:
end *IMPROVE;*

```
    procedure SINGULAR(why);
      value why; integer why;
      comment Prints error messages for DECOMPOSE and
              IMPROVE;
      comment outstring means write;
    begin
      if why = 0 then
        outstring('Matrix with zero row in DECOMPOSE.');
      if why = 1 then
        outstring('Singular matrix in DECOMPOSE.  SOLVE will
              divide by zero.');
      if why = 2 then
        outstring('No convergence in IMPROVE. Matrix is nearly
              singular.');
    end SINGULAR;
  end Linear system package, ALGOL 60 version
```

Notes on the ALGOL *program:* $DECOMPOSE$ (n, A, LU) uses elimination to find n-by-n triangular matrices L and U so that $LU = PA$, where PA is the matrix A with its rows interchanged. The interchange information is stored in the global array ps, and the matrices $L - I$ and U are stored in LU.

$SOLVE$ (n, LU, b, x) uses the LU factorization from $DECOMPOSE$ to find an approximate solution to a single system of equations, $Ax = b$.

$IMPROVE$ $(n, A, LU, b, x, digits)$ requires a copy of the original matrix A, its LU decomposition, a right-hand side b, and the approximate solution x computed by $SOLVE$. It carries out the iterative improvement process until, if possible, x is accurate to machine precision. It also provides an estimate $digits$ of the accuracy of the first approximation. The value of $digits$ is, roughly, the number of decimal digits of x which are not changed by the iteration. This is a measure of the condition of A.

$SINGULAR$ (why) is used by the other procedures to indicate the occurrence of an error condition.

In practice, these procedures are used by another procedure or executive program written to handle a specific class of problems. As an example, we have included in Sec. 18 a procedure which inverts a matrix.

$DECOMPOSE$ uses elimination, basically in the form described in Sec. 9. Temporarily ignoring scaling and pivoting, we can express the central calculation, the elimination, by

(16.2)   **for** $j := k + 1$ **step** 1 **until** n **do**

$$a_{i,j} := a_{i,j} - (a_{i,k}/a_{k,k}) \times a_{k,j}.$$

This operation is carried out by the innermost FOR statement. The multipliers, i.e., the factors $a_{i,k}/a_{k,k}$, are saved because they form the lower triangular matrix L.

The importance of proper scaling or equilibration was pointed out in Sec. 11. It was shown there that the only possible effect of the scaling is to alter the choice of the pivots. Therefore in *DECOMPOSE* we find an element of largest absolute value in each row of the matrix and record its reciprocal in *scales* but do not actually carry out any scaling. Instead, these scale factors are used for choosing the pivot element and only for that. This technique has two favorable consequences: We do not need to use exact powers of the machine base for scaling, and the scale factors do not have to be applied to the right-hand sides.

The same type of consideration is involved in pivoting. The global array *ps* is initialized so that $ps[i] = i$. During the elimination the largest element in the column is chosen as the pivot element, but the rows (equations) are not actually interchanged. The corresponding elements of *ps* are interchanged instead. We then refer to $A[ps[i], j]$ instead of $A[i, j]$. This involves no great loss in time as long as all "inner loops" are on the column subscript j. We gain the time that would be required to carry out the interchange.

This pivoting scheme can be interpreted in two ways. To illustrate, assume that $n = 5$ and that upon return from *DECOMPOSE* the vector $ps = (3, 5, 1, 2, 4)$. The values stored in the array LU can be separated into two parts, which we represent schematically as follows:

$$\begin{bmatrix} m & m & u & u & u \\ m & m & m & u & u \\ u & u & u & u & u \\ m & m & m & m & u \\ m & u & u & u & u \end{bmatrix}.$$

These represent two matrices

$$L_* = \begin{bmatrix} m & m & 1 & 0 & 0 \\ m & m & m & 1 & 0 \\ 1 & 0 & 0 & 0 & 0 \\ m & m & m & m & 1 \\ m & 1 & 0 & 0 & 0 \end{bmatrix} \quad \text{and} \quad U_* = \begin{bmatrix} 0 & 0 & u & u & u \\ 0 & 0 & 0 & u & u \\ u & u & u & u & u \\ 0 & 0 & 0 & 0 & u \\ 0 & u & u & u & u \end{bmatrix}.$$

Then we have $$L_* U_* = A.$$

Of course, the matrices L_* and U_* are not triangular, but they are of such a form that the equations $L_* y = b$ and $U_* x = y$ can be easily solved.

Alternatively, let P be the permutation matrix

$$P = \begin{bmatrix} 0 & 0 & 1 & 0 & 0 \\ 0 & 0 & 0 & 0 & 1 \\ 1 & 0 & 0 & 0 & 0 \\ 0 & 1 & 0 & 0 & 0 \\ 0 & 0 & 0 & 1 & 0 \end{bmatrix}$$

and let L and U be L_* and U_* with the rows rearranged to form triangular matrices. Then we have

$$LU = PA.$$

In other words L and U are the factors of a permuted form of A. See theorem (10.3) for a general statement.

Once we have decided to handle the pivoting with a double-indexing scheme instead of with actual interchanges, it becomes more efficient on many machines to use Gaussian elimination rather than Crout's algorithm. Crout involves indexing on both the column and row subscripts in the inner loops. It is not clear at this writing which method is best in general. It may depend upon details of the machine organization.

If a scale factor or pivot element turns out to be zero, then A must be singular. This could be handled by including as another parameter in *DECOMPOSE* an exit label for singular matrices. We have avoided this because such labels are often a programming nuisance for the casual user. Instead we call upon the procedure *SINGULAR* to print out an error message, and return control to *DECOMPOSE*. The user must modify *SINGULAR* if he desires any other action. If the *LU* factorization is later used in *SOLVE* —as is usually the case—then a division by zero will occur. (See Sec. 15 for our discussion of singular systems.)

DECOMPOSE may be used in two ways. The statement

$$DECOMPOSE(n, A, LU)$$

causes the factors of A to be stored in *LU*. The array A itself is not altered but is saved for use in subsequent calculations, such as iterative improvement. However, saving A requires two n-by-n arrays, A and *LU*. The statement

$$DECOMPOSE(n, A, A)$$

causes the factors to be stored in A itself, thereby destroying the original matrix. This conserves storage if A is no longer needed.

It is relatively simple to calculate determinants using the *LU* decom-position. Care must be taken to avoid exponent underflow and overflow, and the pivoting must be considered when ascertaining the sign of the determinant. See Sec. 14 and exercise (16.5).

SOLVE has an easy job because almost all the work has been done by *DECOMPOSE*. *SOLVE* consists of two statements. The first solves the lower triangular system $Ly = b$. The second is the back solution, i.e., the solution of the upper triangular system $Ux = y$. The intermediate vector y is stored in x, and the right-hand side b is not altered. Since *SOLVE* needs the pivoting information, the array *ps* is declared at the same level as the basic procedures and is global to them.

IMPROVE attempts to improve the solution found by *SOLVE*. The residuals r are calculated using *accumdotprod*. Then the corrections dx are found using *SOLVE* and are added to x. This process is iterated until, roughly, the change in x is less than the precision of the computer system or until the upper limit on the number of iterations is reached.

The criteria for stopping iterations such as this are always difficult to specify. We have chosen the following: The norm, called *normx*, of the first solution is calculated. The norm $\max_i |x_i|$ is used rather than the euclidean norm (see Sec. 2) because it is faster to calculate and behaves in essentially the same way. The norm *normdx* of the actual change made by adding dx to x is also calculated at each iteration. When the relative change in x, that is *normdx/normx*, becomes less than some small number, the iteration is assumed to have converged. The small number *eps* is the unit round-off of the machine; it will be defined in (20.9). Basically, it is the largest number for which

$$1.0 + eps = 1.0$$

is true in the floating arithmetic of the machine. This value is machine de-pendent and must be supplied in any particular implementation.

The value *itmax* for the maximum number of iterations is taken to be twice the number of decimal digits in a floating-point number, although this is somewhat arbitrary. It is also machine dependent. If this maximum is reached, then A must be so ill conditioned that the original x and all dx's probably have less than "half a digit" correct.

If less than full machine accuracy is desired for x, then *eps* can be set to a larger value. It may even be desirable in certain applications to make *eps* a parameter of *IMPROVE* so that the accuracy of different solutions can be controlled.

The parameter *digits*, which is given the value of $-\log_{10}(normdx/normx)$ for the first correction, is an indication of the number of correct (decimal) digits in the x calculated by *SOLVE*. If x is the correct answer, then $dx = \theta$

and *digits* should be infinite. If x has errors on the order of units in the last place, then dx is about the size of these errors and *digits* is approximately the number of digits in the floating-point word. On the other hand, if A is so badly conditioned that dx is roughly the same size as x, then *digits* can be close to zero or even negative. The considerations outlined in Sec. 13 show that the condition cond (A) can be roughly estimated by

$$\text{cond } (A) = \frac{1}{eps} \frac{normdx}{normx}$$

(16.3)

$$= (1/eps) \cdot 10^{-digits}$$

It is essential that the residuals be accurate. The i-th component of the residuals,

$$r_i = b_i - \sum_{j=1}^{n} a_{i,j} x_j,$$

is calculated by the procedure *accumdotprod*. We expect the sum

$$\sum_{j=1}^{n} a_{i,j} x_j$$

to be very close to the value of the b_i so that their difference is very small. If the sum is evaluated with ordinary single-precision arithmetic, then almost all significance will be lost in the final subtraction. The best way to calculate the residuals is to use an *accumulated inner product*. The ordinary multiplication of the two single-precision numbers $a_{i,j}$ and x_j produces a double-precision value. The sum of these double-precision terms should be calculated using double-precision additions. Finally this double-precision sum should be subtracted from b_i using a double-precision subtraction. This complete operation can be done quite efficiently on some computers, but on others it requires elaborate, lengthy coding. In any case, the calculation cannot be completely expressed in ALGOL 60 and it is necessary to use some extension of ALGOL or machine code for the body of *accumdotprod*. We will discuss accumulated inner products in more detail in Sec. 20 and, for some specific computers, in the next section.

In both *DECOMPOSE* and *SOLVE* most of the arithmetic is done in *inner loops*. These are FOR statements involving the variable j. If a given ALGOL translator does not produce efficient programs, it may be desirable to use extensions of the language or machine code to obtain greater speed in these loops.

In presenting these procedures, we have chosen from several possible variations. In doing so, we have attempted to give programs which are easily understood by readers and reasonably efficient in most computer systems. For example, if Crout's method with accumulated inner products were used to calculate L and U then *DECOMPOSE* would require more time, but *IMPROVE* might require less. The total time difference would depend upon the actual problem being solved and the details of the inner-product computation. Furthermore, the choice between double row indexing and actual interchanges would depend upon the subscripting techniques used by the particular compiler.

Ralston (1965) also discusses the implementation of various methods. ALGOL programs are given by Bowdler, Martin, Peters, and Wilkinson (1966).

(16.4) **Exercise.** Implement and test these procedures on a computer, making whatever changes are necessary for the particular ALGOL system that is available. In particular, provide the body of the procedure *accumdotprod* and the appropriate values for *eps* and *itmax*.

(16.5) **Exercise.** Write a procedure *DETERMINANT* (*n*, *LU*, *logdet*, *signdet*) which uses the *LU* factorization from *DECOMPOSE* to evaluate the logarithm and the sign of the determinant of the matrix. (See Sec. 14.) If convenient, you may modify *DECOMPOSE* to keep track of the sign changes caused by interchanges, or the sign information can be obtained from *ps*.

(16.6) **Exercise.** Make the necessary changes to *IMPROVE* so that the iteration is immediately terminated if *digits* is found to be less than some predetermined quantity. What is an appropriate value for this quantity, and what is its relation to *eps* and *itmax*? Should *SINGULAR* be used here?

17. FORTRAN, EXTENDED ALGOL, AND PL/I PROGRAMS

The procedures in the previous section can, for the most part, be translated directly into other algorithmic computer languages. We do this here with an accepted standardization of FORTRAN, a particular implementation of an extended ALGOL, and a preliminary specification of PL/I. Each program illustrates points about the procedures themselves and about the languages and computers used. (The reader is invited to skip the material involving languages or computers with which he is not familiar.)

The FORTRAN language we use is, we believe, that described in American Standards Association (1964) and commonly called ASA FORTRAN. It includes, as far as possible, the common features of three FORTRAN dialects: FORTRAN IV for the IBM 7090/94, FORTRAN 63 for the CDC 1604, and Basic Programming Support FORTRAN for the IBM System/360; see International Business Machines (1965a), Control Data Corp. (1963), and International Business Machines (1965b), respectively. We have avoided features like type declarations, relational expressions, labeled common storage, and adjustable array dimensions, which would be useful but which have different forms or do not exist in one or more of the systems. Some minor incompatibilities still exist: the form of the double-precision declaration in IMPRUV; the spelling of the function names ABS, AMAX1, and ALOG10 in DECOMP and IMPRUV; and the output unit number in SING. With possible changes at these points, the subroutines should also work with other FORTRAN systems.

(17.1)   FORTRAN program for solving a linear system

```
      SUBROUTINE DECOMP (NN, A, UL)
      DIMENSION A(30,30), UL(30,30), SCALES(30), IPS(30)
      COMMON IPS
      N = NN
C
C     INITIALIZE IPS, UL AND SCALES
      DO 5 I = 1,N
        IPS(I) = I
        ROWNRM = 0.0
        DO 2 J = 1,N
          UL(I,J) = A(I,J)
          IF(ROWNRM-ABS(UL(I,J))) 1,2,2
    1     ROWNRM = ABS(UL(I,J))
    2   CONTINUE
        IF (ROWNRM) 3,4,3
    3   SCALES(I) = 1.0/ROWNRM
        GO TO 5
    4   CALL SING(1)
        SCALES(I) = 0.0
    5 CONTINUE
```

```
C
C       GAUSSIAN ELIMINATION WITH PARTIAL PIVOTING
        NM1 = N-1
        DO 17 K = 1,NM1
            BIG = 0.0
            DO 11 I = K,N
                IP = IPS(I)
                SIZE = ABS(UL(IP,K))*SCALES(IP)
                IF (SIZE-BIG) 11,11,10
        10          BIG = SIZE
                    IDXPIV = I
        11      CONTINUE
            IF (BIG) 13,12,13
        12      CALL SING(2)
                GO TO 17
        13      IF (IDXPIV-K) 14,15,14
        14      J = IPS(K)
                IPS(K) = IPS(IDXPIV)
                IPS(IDXPIV) = J
        15      KP = IPS(K)
                PIVOT = UL(KP,K)
                KP1 = K+1
                DO 16 I = KP1,N
                    IP = IPS(I)
                    EM = -UL(IP,K)/PIVOT
                    UL(IP,K) = -EM
                    DO 16 J = KP1,N
                        UL(IP,J) = UL(IP,J) + EM*UL(KP,J)
C                       INNER LOOP.  USE MACHINE LANGUAGE CODING IF COMPILER
C                       DOES NOT PRODUCE EFFICIENT CODE.
        16      CONTINUE
        17 CONTINUE
        KP = IPS(N)
        IF (UL(KP,N)) 19,18,19
        18 CALL SING(2)
        19 RETURN
        END
```

```
        SUBROUTINE SOLVE (NN, UL, B, X)
        DIMENSION UL(30,30), B(30), X(30), IPS(30)
        COMMON IPS
        N = NN
        NP1 = N+1
C
        IP = IPS(1)
        X(1) = B(IP)
        DO 2 I = 2,N
            IP = IPS(I)
            IM1 = I-1
            SUM = 0.0
            DO 1 J = 1,IM1
        1       SUM = SUM + UL(IP,J)*X(J)
        2 X(I) = B(IP) - SUM
C
        IP = IPS(N)
        X(N) = X(N)/UL(IP,N)
        DO 4 IBACK = 2,N
        I = NP1-IBACK
C           I GOES (N-1),...,1
            IP = IPS(I)
            IP1 = I+1
            SUM = 0.0
            DO 3 J = IP1,N
        3       SUM = SUM + UL(IP,J)*X(J)
        4 X(I) = (X(I)-SUM)/UL(IP,I)
        RETURN
        END
```

```
      SUBROUTINE IMPRUV (NN, A, UL, B, X, DIGITS)
      DIMENSION A(30,30), UL(30,30), B(30), X(30), R(30), DX(30)
C     USES ABS(), AMAX1(), ALOG10()
      DOUBLE PRECISION SUM
      N = NN
C
      EPS = 1.0E-8
      ITMAX = 16
C     *** EPS AND ITMAX ARE MACHINE DEPENDENT. ***
C
      XNORM = 0.0
      DO 1 I = 1,N
    1    XNORM = AMAX1(XNORM,ABS(X(I)))
      IF (XNORM) 3,2,3
    2    DIGITS = -ALOG10(EPS)
         GO TO 10
C
    3 DO 9 ITER = 1,ITMAX
         DO 5 I = 1,N
            SUM = 0.0
            DO 4 J = 1,N
    4          SUM = SUM + A(I,J)*X(J)
            SUM = B(I) - SUM
    5       R(I) = SUM
C     *** IT IS ESSENTIAL THAT A(I,J)*X(J) YIELD A DOUBLE PRECISION
C           RESULT AND THAT THE ABOVE + AND - BE DOUBLE PRECISION.  ***
         CALL SOLVE (N,UL,R,DX)
         DXNORM = 0.0
         DO 6 I = 1,N
            T = X(I)
            X(I) = X(I) + DX(I)
            DXNORM = AMAX1(DXNORM,ABS(X(I)-T))
    6       CONTINUE
         IF (ITER-1) 8,7,8
    7       DIGITS = -ALOG10(AMAX1(DXNORM/XNORM,EPS))
    8       IF (DXNORM-EPS*XNORM) 10,10,9
    9 CONTINUE
C     ITERATION DID NOT CONVERGE
      CALL SING(3)
   10 RETURN
      END
```

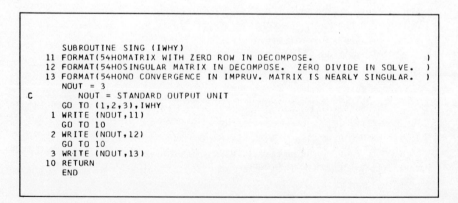

```
      SUBROUTINE SING (IWHY)
   11 FORMAT(54HOMATRIX WITH ZERO ROW IN DECOMPOSE.                    )
   12 FORMAT(54HOSINGULAR MATRIX IN DECOMPOSE.   ZERO DIVIDE IN SOLVE.  )
   13 FORMAT(54HONO CONVERGENCE IN IMPRUV. MATRIX IS NEARLY SINGULAR.   )
      NOUT = 3
C     NOUT = STANDARD OUTPUT UNIT
      GO TO (1,2,3),IWHY
    1 WRITE (NOUT,11)
      GO TO 10
    2 WRITE (NOUT,12)
      GO TO 10
    3 WRITE (NOUT,13)
   10 RETURN
      END
```

Note that the *LU* of the ALGOL programs is expressed by *UL* in our FORTRAN programs.

It may require several FORTRAN statements to express a single ALGOL statement, particularly those involving subscripts and logical or Boolean constructions. But the compiler may, in some sense, compensate for this by producing more efficient machine code. This is particularly true in our case. In FORTRAN the inner loop in DECOMP is

(17.2)
$$\text{DO } 16 \text{ J} = \text{KP1,N}$$
$$16 \quad \text{UL(IP, J)} = \text{UL(IP, J)} + \text{EM*UL(KP, J)}$$

On the 7090, the resulting machine code consists of only seven instructions: a load, a multiply, an add, a store, and three indexing instructions. All operations that do not depend upon J are done outside the loop. The inner loops in SOLVE are handled in a similar manner.

In all three subroutines the 7090 and 1604 compilers were able to produce near-perfect machine code. This is due partly to the detail with which it is necessary to state the algorithms in FORTRAN and partly to the rather elaborate techniques these particular compilers use to produce efficient code. One may question in many situations whether the extra time required by the programmer and the compiler to achieve this is justified. In the case of subroutines such as these which will be used many times without change, we feel that it is.

The special procedure *accumdotprod* is not needed in our FORTRAN version of *IMPROVE*. The accumulated inner product is obtained by declaring SUM to be a double-precision variable. The statements

(17.3)
$$\text{DOUBLE PRECISION SUM}$$
$$\text{SUM} = \text{SUM} + \text{A(I, J)*X(J)}$$

should produce a double-length value for the product and add this to SUM with a double-precision addition. However, this is accomplished in rather different ways on different machines.

On the 7090 and 7094 a floating-point multiply instruction produces a double-length result in two registers (the accumulator and the multiplier-quotient registers). A double-precision floating-point addition adds such a number to another double-length number stored in two memory locations. So the statements in (17.3) result in a single-precision multiplication, a double-precision addition, and a double-precision store. This is exactly what we mean by an accumulated inner product. (Double-precision addition is a hardware instruction on the 7094 and is accomplished with four single-precision additions on the 7090.)

The CDC 1604 automatically rounds after each floating-point operation. This is desirable in almost all contexts but this one. In order to obtain the double-length value of the product and to perform the double-precision addition it becomes necessary to use special subroutines which "unpack" the floating-point numbers and perform arithmetic using fixed-point operations. This means that the iterative improvement is rather costly relative to the triangular decomposition. But limiting the double-precision work to the relatively small amount of arithmetic needed for iterative improvement is much more desirable than doing the entire computation with double-precision arithmetic, to achieve, perhaps, the same final accuracy.

Our experience with the IBM System/360 is limited but demonstrates yet another situation. The 360 has two lengths of floating-point numbers— the "short form" and the "long form," which is more than twice as precise as the short form. A short-form floating-point multiplication yields a long-form result. If this can be followed by a long-form addition, we have our accumulated inner product. However, the preliminary compiler we used truncated the product to short form before doing the addition. In this situation it was necessary to replace (17.3) with

$$DOUBLE \ PRECISION \ SUM, \ AIJ, \ XJ$$

$$AIJ = A(I, J)$$

$$XJ = X(J)$$

$$SUM = SUM + AIJ*XJ$$

Future versions of the compiler may improve this situation.

We have gone into detail on these points for several reasons. They illustrate how features of different computers and compiler systems may affect the accuracy and efficiency of a particular algorithm. They also point out the need for standardization—the program segment (17.3) was acceptable to all three compilers but produced different results in each case. Finally, it is unfortunately true that anyone who desires to use these programs on a particular computer will also have to face these or similar problems.

For other FORTRAN IV linear equation solvers we call attention to excellent programs by Kahan (1965b). These make full use of the University of Toronto's modifications of the FORTRAN monitor to recover from over- and underflow.

The version of ALGOL we used was Extended ALGOL for the Burroughs B5500 (Burroughs (1964)). We have not reproduced the complete program listing here because it is almost identical to the ALGOL 60 program in Sec. 16. (A left arrow ← is substituted for the replacement operator := ; the lower subscript bounds of the parametric arrays must be specified; and the labels must be declared. Also, the declaration of the procedure *SINGULAR* must be placed ahead of that of *DECOMPOSE*. The lower bounds of all arrays are specified to be zero since this produces faster code.) However, we wish to describe two useful extensions of ALGOL available in the Burroughs system—the "array-row" feature and the "double" statement.

The array-row feature is used in all the procedures except *SINGULAR* to increase efficiency. For fixed i, as the index j varies, the quantity $A[i, j]$ acts like a one-dimensional array. This one-dimensional row is denoted by A[I, *] and can be used as an actual parameter of any procedure statement in which the corresponding formal parameter is specified to be a one-dimensional array. In the execution of this procedure, then, subscripting is quite efficient. For example, the statement

> **if** *mult* $\neq 0$ **then**
>
> **for** $j := k + 1$ **step** 1 **until** n **do**
>
> $LU[ps[i], j] := LU[ps[i], j] - mult \times LU[ps[k], j]$

in the ALGOL 60 version of *DECOMPOSE* is replaced by

> IF MULT $\neq 0$ THEN
>
> ELIM(K + 1, N, MULT, LU[PS[I], *], LU[PS[K], *])

in the Burroughs Extended ALGOL version. The declaration of the procedure ELIM is

```
PROCEDURE ELIM (J1, J2, MULT, AI, AK);
    VALUE J1, J2, MULT; INTEGER J1, J2; REAL MULT;
    REAL ARRAY AI, AK [0];
BEGIN INTEGER J;
    FOR J ← J1 STEP 1 UNTIL J2 DO
    AI[J] ← AI[J] − MULT × AK[J];
END ELIM;
```

A similar change is made in the FOR statements involving j in *SOLVE*. Both procedures work without these changes; the changes only increase the speed.

The double statements are necessary to calculate the residual vector. A double statement consists of a sequence of double-precision operators and operands in so-called suffix Polish notation. We do not wish to explain this in much detail here. Suffice it to say that the statement

DOUBLE (X[J], 0, Y[J], 0, ×, SUMHI, SUMLO, +, ←, SUMHI, SUMLO)

is a double-precision version of

$$\text{SUM} \leftarrow \text{SUM} + X[J] \times Y[J].$$

This is used with the array-row feature to compute the residuals. The pertinent parts of the program are

        FOR I ← 1 STEP 1 UNTIL N DO
            R[I] ← −DOUBLEDOTPROD(1, N, A[I, *], X, − B[I]);
and

REAL PROCEDURE DOUBLEDOTPROD (J1, J2, X, Y, C);
    VALUE J1, J2, C; INTEGER J1, J2; REAL C; REAL ARRAY X, Y[0];
BEGIN INTEGER J; REAL SUMHI, SUMLO;
    SUMHI ← SUMLO ← 0;
    FOR J ← J1 STEP 1 UNTIL J2 DO
    DOUBLE (X[J], 0, Y[J], 0, ×, SUMHI, SUMLO, +, ←,
                                        SUMHI, SUMLO);
    DOUBLE (SUMHI, SUMLO, C, 0, +, ←, SUMHI, SUMLO);
    DOUBLEDOTPROD ← SUMHI;
END DOUBLEDOTPROD;

Note that it is necessary to perform a double-precision multiplication as well as the double-precision addition.

At the time of this writing the future status of the PL/I language is not clear. However, since PL/I may become an important computer language, we include PL/I versions of our programs in this section. These programs have been run successfully, but changes may be necessary to comply with future language specifications. The programs are given in terms of the 60-character language as defined in International Business Machines (1966).

(17.4)   **Exercise.**   Do exercises (16.4), (16.5), and (16.6), using the language and the computer available to you.

(17.5)   PL/I program for solving a linear system

```
DECOMPOSE: PROCEDURE (N, A, LU) ;
  DECLARE A(*,*)  /* MATRIX TO BE DECOMPOSED */,
          LU(*,*) FLOAT  /* RESULTS */ ;
  DECLARE PS(100) FIXED BINARY EXTERNAL  /* PIVOT VECTOR, N<=100 */,
          SCALES (N), (MULT, NORMROW, BIGGEST, SIZE, PIVOT) FLOAT,
          (I, J, K, PIVIDX) FIXED BINARY ;
  /* INITIALIZE PS, LU AND SCALES */
  DO I = 1 TO N ;
    PS(I) = I ;
    NORMROW = 0 ;
    DO J = 1 TO N ;
      LU(I,J) = A(I,J) ;
      NORMROW = MAX(NORMROW, ABS(LU(I,J))) ;
    END ;
    IF NORMROW ¬= 0 THEN SCALES(I) = 1.0/NORMROW ;
    ELSE DO;  SCALES(I) = 0;  CALL SINGULAR('ROW');    END ;
  END ;
  /* GAUSSIAN ELIMINATION WITH PARTIAL PIVOTING */
  DO K = 1 TO N-1 ;
    BIGGEST = 0 ;
    DO I = K TO N ;
      SIZE = ABS(LU(PS(I),K))*SCALES(PS(I)) ;
      IF SIZE > BIGGEST THEN
          DO; BIGGEST = SIZE;  PIVIDX = I;  END ;
    END ;
    IF BIGGEST = 0 THEN
        DO; CALL SINGULAR('PIV'); GO TO ENDKLOOP;  END ;
    IF PIVIDX ¬= K THEN
        DO;  J = PS(K);  PS(K) = PS(PIVIDX); PS(PIVIDX) = J;  END ;
    PIVOT = LU(PS(K),K) ;
    DO I = K+1 TO N ;
      LU(PS(I),K) , MULT = LU(PS(I),K)/PIVOT ;
      IF MULT ¬= 0 THEN
          DO J = K+1 TO N ;
            LU(PS(I),J) = LU(PS(I),J) - MULT*LU(PS(K),J) ;
            /* INNER LOOP.  ROW SUBSCRIPTS DON'T VARY */
          END ;
    END ;
  ENDKLOOP:
  END ;
  IF LU(PS(N),N) = 0 THEN CALL SINGULAR('PIV') ;
  END DECOMPOSE ;
```

```
SOLVE: PROCEDURE (N, LU, B, X) ;
  DECLARE LU(*,*) FLOAT  /* DECOMPOSITION OF A */ ,
          B(*)  /* RIGHT HAND SIDE */ ,
          X(*)  /* SOLUTION */ ;
  DECLARE PS(100) FIXED BINARY EXTERNAL  /* PIVOT VECTOR, N<=100 */,
          DOT FLOAT, (I, J) FIXED BINARY ;
  DO I = 1 TO N ;
    DOT = 0 ;
    DO J = 1 TO I-1 ;
      DOT = DOT + LU(PS(I),J)*X(J) ;
    END ;
    X(I) = B(PS(I)) - DOT ;
  END ;
  DO I = N TO 1 BY -1 ;
    DOT = 0 ;
    DO J = I+1 TO N ;
      DOT = DOT + LU(PS(I),J)*X(J) ;
    END ;
    X(I) = (X(I) - DOT)/LU(PS(I),I) ;
  END ;
  END SOLVE ;
```

```
IMPROVE: PROCEDURE (N, A, LU, B, X, DIGITS) ;
  DECLARE A(*,*)  /* ORIGINAL MATRIX */ ,
          LU(*,*) FLOAT  /* DECOMPOSITION OF A */ ,
          B(*)  /* RIGHT HAND SIDE */ ,
          X(*)  /* APPROXIMATE SOLUTION TO BE IMPROVED */ ,
          DIGITS  /* WILL BE SET TO ACCURACY OF INPUT X */ ;

  DECLARE (R,DX) (N), (NORMX, NORMDX, T) FLOAT,
          (I, J, ITER) FIXED BINARY,
          EPS INITIAL (1.E-6)  /* MACHINE DEPENDENT ROUNDOFF LEVEL */,
          ITMAX INITIAL (12)  /* USE 2*LOG10(1/EPS) APPROXIMATELY */ ;

  DECLARE DPSUM FLOAT (12)
  /* IT IS ESSENTIAL THAT PRECISION OF DPSUM AND ARGUMENT OF MULTIPLY
     USED BELOW BE TWICE DEFAULT PRECISION.  DEFAULT PRECISION OF 6
     ASSUMED HERE. */ ;

  NORMX = 0 ;
  DO I = 1 TO N ;
     NORMX = MAX(NORMX,ABS(X(I))) ;
  END ;
  IF NORMX = 0 THEN
     DO;  DIGITS = -LOG10(EPS); GO TO CONVERGED;  END ;

  DO ITER = 1 TO ITMAX ;
     DO I = 1 TO N ;
        DPSUM = 0 ;
        DO J = 1 TO N ;
           DPSUM = DPSUM + MULTIPLY(A(I,J), X(J), 12) ;
        END ;
        DPSUM = B(I) - DPSUM ;
        R(I) = DPSUM :
     END ;
     CALL SOLVE(N,LU,R,DX) ;
     NORMDX = 0 ;
     DO I = 1 TO N ;
        T = X(I) ;
        X(I) = X(I) + DX(I) ;
        NORMDX = MAX(NORMDX,ABS(X(I)-T)) ;
     END ;
     IF ITER = 1 THEN DIGITS = -LOG10(MAX(NORMDX/NORMX,EPS)) ;
     IF NORMDX <= EPS*NORMX THEN GO TO CONVERGED ;
  END ;
  CALL SINGULAR('CON') ;
  CONVERGED:
  END IMPROVE ;
```

```
SINGULAR: PROCEDURE (WHY) ;
  DECLARE WHY CHARACTER(3) ;
  IF WHY='ROW' THEN PUT SKIP(2) LIST
     ('ZERO ROW IN DECOMPOSE') ;
  IF WHY='PIV' THEN PUT SKIP(2) LIST
     ('SINGULAR MATRIX IN DECOMPOSE. SOLVE WILL DIVIDE BY ZERO.') ;
  IF WHY='CON' THEN PUT SKIP(2) LIST
     ('NO CONVERGENCE IN IMPROVE. MATRIX IS NEARLY SINGULAR.') ;
  END SINGULAR ;
```

18. MATRIX INVERSION

One way to solve the system of linear equations $Ax = b$ is to compute the inverse of A and then multiply A^{-1} by b. This method may appear especially attractive if several right-hand sides b_k are involved since the inverse need be computed only once. However, a set of linear equation solving procedures—such as *DECOMPOSE* and *SOLVE*—can accomplish this task with fewer operations and with greater accuracy. Once L and U have been computed, the solution of $LUx = b$ requires $n^2 - n$ multiplications and n divisions or a total of n^2 multiplicative operations; see exercise (9.5). Moreover, once A^{-1} has been computed, the evaluation of $A^{-1}b$ requires n^2 multiplicative operations also. Thus both methods require approximately the same number of operations at this point. But the initial calculations of LU and of A^{-1} require about $\frac{1}{3}n^3$ and n^3 multiplicative operations, respectively. Thus using LU is faster than using A^{-1}, even if many right-hand sides are involved. Furthermore, because there are fewer operations and hence fewer rounding errors, the use of LU can be expected to give more accurate results in most cases.

However, there are applications in which A^{-1} is wanted for reasons other than solving linear systems. In these situations the inversion of the matrix can be accomplished very easily by using the procedures for solving linear equations. The columns of A^{-1} are simply the respective solutions of the n different linear systems

$$Ax_1 = e_1, Ax_2 = e_2, \ldots, Ax_n = e_n.$$

Here e_i is the i-th unit vector whose coordinates are all zero except for the i-th, which is one. Hence one need only call the linear equation solver n times with the right-hand sides $e_1, e_2, \ldots, e_n$ in order to invert the matrix. In addition, iterative improvement of each column can be done if desired. Program (18.1) on the next page illustrates how this can be carried out easily using the procedures *DECOMPOSE*, *SOLVE*, and *IMPROVE*.

Sometimes the inverse of a matrix must be obtained without storing essentially more than n^2 elements at any time, In these cases A can be transformed into A^{-1} within the n^2 storage cells of A alone. The method is roughly this: The identity matrix does not need to be stored at all. As Gaussian elimination proceeds, elements of A are made zero at the same rate as new elements are introduced on the right-hand side. Thus, the newly created elements of the transformed identity matrix are stored in place of the zeroed elements of A. This is often done in a compact arrangement which is fairly difficult to understand. However, many of these procedures suffer because there is no searching for pivots. Moreover, since A is destroyed during the

(18.1)　　　　　　　ALGOL 60 procedure to invert a matrix

```
procedure INVERT(n, A, AINV);
  value n; integer n; real array A, AINV;
  comment Example of the use of DECOMPOSE, SOLVE, and
          IMPROVE to invert a matrix;
begin
  real array LU[1:n, 1:n], b, x[1:n];
  integer i, j; real digits;
  DECOMPOSE(n, A, LU);
  for j := 1 step 1 until n do
  begin
    for i := 1 step 1 until n do
      b[i] := if i = j then 1 else 0;
    SOLVE(n, LU, b, x);
    IMPROVE(n, A, LU, b, x, digits);
      comment digits is ignored;
      for i := 1 step 1 until n do AINV[i, j] := x[i];
  end;
end INVERT;
```

inversion, it is not possible to carry out any iterative improvement. If a separate copy of A is saved for the improvement process, one loses the main advantage of the compact arrangement—the conservation of storage.

If the computation is arranged especially for inversion, with or without a search for pivots, it takes approximately n^3 multiplications to obtain a first inverse. This inverse—for example, X_0—can be improved by using techniques analogous to those given above for linear systems. For $k = 0$, $1, 2, \ldots$, let $R_k = I - AX_k$ be the residual matrix corresponding to A^{-1}. Then, if X_k is a good approximation of A^{-1}, we expect that $X_k R_k$ is close to $A^{-1} R_k = A^{-1} - X_k$. The latter is just what should be added to X_k to yield A^{-1}. Hence we use $X_k + X_k R_k$ as the next approximate inverse, called X_{k+1}.

In summary, the iteration

$$X_{k+1} := X_k + X_k(I - AX_k)$$

appears likely to furnish a rapidly improving inverse. In proof (ignoring round-off) it is easily shown that

$$I - AX_{k+1} = (I - AX_k)^2.$$

Hence, if
$$\|I - AX_0\| = \epsilon < 1,$$

we see that
$$\|I - AX_1\| \leq \epsilon^2$$

and that
$$\|I - AX_k\| \leq \epsilon^{2^k}.$$

Since this expression goes to zero quadratically as $k \to \infty$, in exact, real arithmetic the iteration is rapidly convergent. It is often called Newton's process because its scalar analog,

$$x_{k+1} := x_k + x_k(1 - ax_k),$$

is precisely Newton's process for solving the equation

$$f(x) = a - (1/x) = 0.$$

Newton's matrix iteration is frequently written in the form

$$X_{k+1} := X_k(2I - AX_k).$$

As a result of the discussion of iterative improvement in Sec. 13, the reader should doubt that a single-precision iteration in this form will lead to an accurate single-precision inverse if the matrix A is ill conditioned. Like iterative improvement, this Newton matrix iteration leads to high accuracy only when the residual $R_k = I - AX_k$ is computed with an accumulated inner product and when the correction $X_k(I - AX_k)$ is separately computed and then added to X_k.

  It should be mentioned that the analogy to Newton's process does not apply to the iterative-improvement process for a single linear system since in the latter we roughly have

$$x_{k+1} := x_k + (LU)^{-1}(b - Ax_k).$$

In terms of Newton's process, the same value of the derivative is used for all iterations. As we shall see later, the error here behaves like ϵ^k instead of ϵ^{2^k}.

  Unless the reader has explicit need for the elements of A^{-1}, we recommend strongly against computing it. As we have said, almost anything you can do with A^{-1} can be done without it.

19. AN EXAMPLE: HILBERT MATRICES

A set of matrices often used—and occasionally misused—as examples in matrix calculations is the set of Hilbert matrices (Hilbert (1894)). One situation in which they occur is the following.

Suppose a continuous function $f(x)$ is given on the interval $0 \leq x \leq 1$ and we are asked to approximate $f(x)$ by a polynomial of degree $n - 1$ in x. We write the polynomial in the form

$$\sum_{i=1}^{n} c_i x^{i-1}$$

and define the error in the approximation to be

$$E = \int_0^1 \left[\sum_{i=1}^{n} c_i x^{i-1} - f(x) \right]^2 dx.$$

The coefficients c_i are to be determined by the requirement that E be minimized. Since the error is a differentiable function of the unknowns c_i, at the minimum

$$\partial E / \partial c_i = 0, \quad i = 1, \ldots, n.$$

Evaluating these derivatives leads to the conditions

$$\frac{\partial E}{\partial c_i} = 2 \int_0^1 \left[\sum_{j=1}^{n} c_j x^{j-1} - f(x) \right] x^{i-1} dx = 0 \quad (i = 1, \ldots, n).$$

Interchanging the summation and integration, we obtain

$$(19.1) \qquad \sum_{j=1}^{n} \left(\int_0^1 x^{i+j-2} dx \right) c_j = \int_0^1 f(x) x^{i-1} dx \quad (i = 1, \ldots, n).$$

These are n equations to be satisfied by the n unknowns c_i. If we let

$$h_{i,j} = \int_0^1 x^{i+j-2} dx = \frac{1}{i+j-1}$$

and

$$b_i = \int_0^1 f(x) x^{i-1} dx \quad (i = 1, \ldots, n),$$

then the equations (19.1) can be written

$$\sum_{j=1}^{n} h_{i,j} c_j = b_i, \quad i = 1, \ldots, n.$$

Thus the column of coefficients $c = (c_1, \ldots, c_n)^T$ can be found by solving the n-by-n system

$$H_n c = b,$$

where the matrix H_n has elements

(19.2) $\qquad h_{i,j} = 1/(i + j - 1), \quad (i, j = 1, \ldots, n)$

and the vector $b = (b_1, \ldots, b_n)^T$ is determined by the given function $f(x)$.

The matrix H_n defined by (19.2) is the n-by-n *Hilbert matrix*. We will let T_n denote its inverse,

(19.3) $\qquad T_n = H_n^{-1}.$

We are primarily interested in the Hilbert matrices because they are very badly conditioned, even for small values of n, and because their condition grows rapidly with increasing n—as table (19.4) shows.

(19.4) $\qquad$ Some information about Hilbert matrices

n	$\|H_n\|$	$\|T_n\|$	cond (H_n)	largest element of T_n
2	1.27	$1.52_{10}1$	$1.93_{10}1$	$1.20_{10}1$
3	1.41	$3.72_{10}2$	$5.24_{10}2$	$1.92_{10}2$
4	1.50	$1.03_{10}4$	$1.55_{10}4$	$6.48_{10}3$
5	1.57	$3.04_{10}5$	$4.77_{10}5$	$1.79_{10}5$
6	1.62	$9.24_{10}6$	$1.50_{10}7$	$4.41_{10}6$
7	1.66	$2.86_{10}8$	$4.75_{10}8$	$1.33_{10}8$
8	1.70	$9.00_{10}9$	$1.53_{10}10$	$4.25_{10}9$
9	1.73	$2.86_{10}11$	$4.93_{10}11$	$1.22_{10}11$
10	1.75	$9.15_{10}12$	$1.60_{10}13$	$3.48_{10}12$

Because they are so poorly conditioned, Hilbert matrices are often used in demonstrations and tests of computer matrix procedures. But, again because they are poorly conditioned, care must be exercised in the way this is done. Let us consider a specific example.

In tables (19.5) through (19.10) we have six six-by-six matrices. All were computed with an IBM 7090, which for purposes of this discussion we may consider as having a relative precision of 10^{-8}. (That is, the value of *eps* in the procedure *IMPROVE* is approximately 10^{-8}.)

(19.5)   Table of $T =$ inverse of six-by-six Hilbert matrix, H

36.00	−630.00	3360.00	−7560.00	7560.00	−2772.00
−630.00	14700.00	−88200.00	211680.00	−220500.00	83160.00
3360.00	−88200.00	564480.00	−1411200.00	1512000.00	−582120.00
−7560.00	211680.00	−1411200.00	3628800.00	−3969000.00	1552320.00
7560.00	−220500.00	1512000.00	−3969000.00	4410000.00	−1746360.00
−2772.00	83160.00	−582120.00	1552320.00	−1746360.00	698544.00

(19.6)   Table of inverse of T, calculated without iterative improvement

1.00018226	.50015343	.33346176	.25010935	.20009571	.16675133
.50019167	.33349262	.25013416	.20011510	.16676722	.14294624
.33351852	.25015344	.20012929	.16677780	.14295436	.12508627
.25017456	.20014443	.16678839	.14296186	.12509169	.11119255
.20016330	.16680165	.14297093	.12509795	.11119693	.10007627
.16681924	.14298318	.12510627	.11120262	.10008021	.09098041

The first matrix, (19.5), is $T_6 = H_6^{-1}$. It was computed by the procedure given in (19.11) and is exact; there are no rounding errors. Its elements are all integers. We have denoted it simply by T, omitting the subscript 6.

The second matrix, (19.6), was obtained by inverting T without using iterative improvement, i.e., using only the procedures *DECOMPOSE* and *SOLVE*. Any other elimination routine would produce approximately the same matrix on a computer with this accuracy. If there were no round-off error we would obtain H. However, the values actually computed are correct to only three or four significant figures because of rounding introduced during the elimination.

(19.7)   Table of inverse of T, calculated with iterative improvement

1.00000000	.49999999	.33333333	.24999999	.20000000	.16666666
.50000000	.33333333	.25000000	.20000000	.16666666	.14285714
.33333333	.24999999	.20000000	.16666666	.14285714	.12500000
.25000000	.20000000	.16666666	.14285714	.12500000	.11111110
.20000000	.16666666	.14285714	.12499999	.11111110	.09999999
.16666666	.14285714	.12500000	.11111110	.09999999	.09090909

(19.8)   Table of $H_* =$ machine approximation of H

1.00000000	.50000000	.33333333	.25000000	.20000000	.16666666
.50000000	.33333333	.25000000	.20000000	.16666666	.14285714
.33333333	.25000000	.20000000	.16666666	.14285714	.12500000
.25000000	.20000000	.16666666	.14285714	.12500000	.11111110
.20000000	.16666666	.14285714	.12500000	.11111110	.09999999
.16666666	.14285714	.12500000	.11111110	.09999999	.09090909 .

(19.9)   Table of T_0 = inverse of H_*, calculated without improvement

36.05	−631.40	3369.20	−7583.47	7585.57	−2781.95
−631.45	14739.81	−88462.34	212349.10	−221227.39	83443.11
3369.79	−88468.85	566250.87	−1415714.73	1516905.83	−584028.87
−7585.42	212377.81	−1415794.56	3640509.72	−3981720.78	1557268.50
7588.01	−221268.61	1517059.27	−3981890.84	4424001.00	−1751805.56
−2783.02	83462.27	−584109.19	1557387.41	−1751862.88	700684.00

(19.10)   Table of T_* = inverse of H_*, calculated with improvement

36.09	−632.59	3377.15	−7603.97	7607.99	−2790.75
−632.59	14771.47	−88673.18	212891.85	−221821.99	83676.11
3377.15	−88673.18	567610.55	−1419212.98	1520737.50	−585529.96
−7603.97	212891.85	−1419212.98	3649301.66	−3991348.19	1561039.56
7607.99	−221821.99	1520737.50	−3991348.19	4434355.06	−1755860.73
−2790.75	83676.11	−585529.96	1561039.56	−1755860.73	702249.59

The third matrix, (19.7), was obtained by using iterative improvement on the matrix of (19.6). The iterative improvement converged to a matrix in which many of the elements have no error at all! The largest relative error is roughly 10^{-8}, which is the round-off level of the machine. Of course, the error must be this small if the procedure *IMPROVE* terminates without an error message. (Actually, the elements of these matrices are binary, not decimal, fractions. Any errors in (19.7) are in the last bit of the floating-point number.) In the calculation of (19.7), the values for *digits* obtained from *IMPROVE* ranged from 3.72 for the first column to 3.27 for the last. These are rather good estimates of the accuracy of the corresponding columns of (19.6).

The fourth matrix, (19.8), was generated directly by the following FORTRAN statements, executed in chopped arithmetic:

```
DO 1 I = 1,N

DO 1 J = 1,N

1 H(I,J) = 1.0/FLOAT(I + J − 1).
```

Thus (19.8) is not the exact Hilbert matrix. It has errors in certain elements, like $h_{1,3} = \frac{1}{3}$, which cannot be exactly represented as decimal or binary fractions. We denote this machine version of H by H_*.

The fifth matrix, (19.9), was obtained by inverting H_* without using iterative improvement; and the sixth matrix, (19.10), was obtained by using improvement on (19.9). Let us denote these two matrices by T_0 and T_*, respectively.

We notice immediately that T_* is very different from T. However (19.10) is the correct inverse of (19.8); that is,

$$T_* = H_*^{-1}$$

to the number of decimal places shown. The convergence proof to be given in Sec. 22 and other calculations confirm that this is true. Thus, all the differences between T and T_* are caused by the differences between H and H_*. If we want to observe the effect of rounding error introduced during the elimination before iterative improvement, we must compare T_0 with T_* and not with T. When this point is overlooked, the Hilbert matrices are being used incorrectly as test matrices.

We see that the differences between T_0 and T_* are actually less than those between T_* and T. That is, the accumulated rounding error introduced during the elimination process used to obtain T_0 has less of an effect than the initial, single rounding error introduced in the generation of the data. This point will be the basis for the discussion and analysis of round-off error in Secs. 20 and 21.

In contrast to representing H_n, no perturbations are necessary in order to represent T_n in the computer, at least for small n, because its elements are all integers. Thus the Hilbert inverses are better examples for studying rounding error than the Hilbert matrices themselves. They can be generated by the procedure in program (19.11) or can be copied from the table given by Savage and Lukacs (1954) and read directly into the computer as data.

However, both H_n and T_n are positive definite matrices, for which it can be shown that pivoting is not necessary. (That is, quite satisfactory error bounds can be obtained for Gaussian elimination without pivoting. Hence changing pivoting strategies is not likely to affect the accuracy.) Consequently, the Hilbert matrices and their inverses should not be used for testing pivoting strategies designed for general matrices. This is a second example of the occasional misuse of Hilbert matrices.

Our six matrices also illustrate an important point about iterative improvement. If the initial data, such as H_n, are subject to error or perturbation, the answer obtained by elimination without improvement is usually as accurate as the data warrant. If instead, the data, like T_n, are exact, it is reasonable to ask for an exact or nearly exact answer. In this latter case iterative improvement is justified and useful.

For a further discussion of Hilbert matrices, see Todd (1954), (1961).

The ill-conditioned nature of the Hilbert matrices can be traced to the approximation problem which we used to introduce them. On the interval $0 \le x \le 1$ the functions x^i ($i = 0, \ldots, n - 1$) are very nearly linearly dependent. This means that the rows of the Hilbert matrix are very nearly linearly dependent, i.e., that the matrix is nearly singular. As we have seen, in these cases small perturbations in the data will result in large perturbations in the answers. In the original problem, small errors in the function $f(x)$ or rounding errors in its calculation can result in large changes in the coefficients c_i. In short, the approximation problem is not "well posed" when it is in a form that leads to a matrix like the Hilbert matrix.

(19.11)   ALGOL program to compute the inverses of the Hilbert matrices

```
procedure Inverse Hilbert (n, T);
value n; integer n; array T;
comment Generates the inverse of the n-by-n Hilbert matrix;
comment Uses integer arithmetic. Result is exact if n is small enough
        so that no overflow occurs. The integer divide ÷ may be
        replaced by / if no rounding error is introduced;
begin
   integer p, r, i, j;
   p := n;
   for i := 1 step 1 until n do
   begin
      if i ≠ 1 then
      p := ((n − i + 1) × p × (n + i − 1)) ÷ (i − 1) ↑ 2;
      r := p ↑ 2;
      T[i, i] := r ÷ (2 × i − 1);
      for j := i + 1 step 1 until n do
      begin
         r := −((n − j + 1) × r × (n + j − 1)) ÷ (j − 1) ↑ 2;
         T[j, i] := T[i, j] := r ÷ (i + j − 1);
      end;
   end;
end Inverse Hilbert;
```

(19.12)   **Exercise.**   Exercise (8.18) shows that

$$\frac{\|T_* - T\|}{\|T_*\|} \leq \text{cond}\,(H)\,\frac{\|H_* - H\|}{\|H\|}\,.$$

Using exercise (2.19) and table (19.4), calculate or estimate the quantities involved in this inequality. Is the inequality sharp? Why?

(19.13)   **Exercise.**   Compute the inverses of T_n and $(H_n)_*$, both with and without iterative improvement. Use as values of n the integers

2, 3, . . . , until the elements of T_n are too large to be represented exactly or until iterative improvement fails to converge. If possible, use a computer with a different word length than the one used in our examples. (Ours was a 7090, which has a 27-bit floating-point significand. The largest invertible Hilbert matrix in this case is $(H_7)_*$.)

(19.14) **Exercise.** Prove that setting the quantities $\partial E/\partial c_i$ equal to zero really does yield a minimum of E in our development at the start of Sec. 19. Also, prove that the solution vector c is a unique minimizing vector for E.

20. FLOATING-POINT ROUND-OFF ANALYSIS

We interrupt our matrix development to present the basis of a round-off analysis for floating-point computations, following Wilkinson (1963), who essentially created the theory. This material will be used in studying the rounding errors which occur in solving linear systems of equations by elimination.

We shall describe one so-called *normalized* floating-point computing system, although others exist. An integer β is chosen as a base, and a number t of base-β digits d_i are devoted to the absolute value of the *significand s* of the number (also called the *fractional part* or *mantissa*). We have seen systems with $\beta = 2, 8, 10,$ and 16; the associated values of t vary greatly. A certain range of integer exponents e is also specified—for example, by $-m \leq e \leq M$. Finally, the number has a sign. Thus any nonzero floating-point number has the form

$$\pm .d_1 d_2 \cdots d_t \times \beta^e,$$

where the integers $d_1, \ldots, d_t, e$ satisfy the inequalities

$$1 \leq d_1 \leq \beta - 1;$$
$$0 \leq d_i \leq \beta - 1, \quad \text{for } i = 2, 3, \ldots, t;$$
$$-m \leq e \leq M.$$

The condition $d_1 \neq 0$ is characteristic of a *normalized* floating-point number. If we let $s = \pm .d_1 d_2 \cdots d_t$, there is an integer N such that

$$|s| = N\beta^{-t} \quad \text{and} \quad \beta^{t-1} \leq N < \beta^t.$$

The floating-point representation of zero is different—usually $s = +0$ and $e = -m$.

On the real number line the floating-point numbers form a finite set $F = F(\beta, t, m, M)$ of far from equidistant points. Figure 20.1 is a schematic representation of the 33 points of F for $\beta = 2, t = 3, m = 1,$ and $M = 2$.

(20.1)   Floating-point numbers for $\beta = 2,\ t = 3,\ m = 1,\ M = 2$

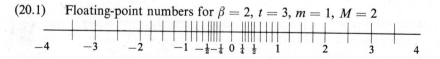

Any real number x that we wish to represent in the computer is approximated by a number in the set F just described—often by the closest number in

F, with some choice in case of a tie. To be specific, given x, we denote by x_R ("x rounded") the closest number in F; in case of a tie we choose x_R as that one of the two closest numbers in F with the larger absolute value. If $x = 0$, then $x_R = 0$. If $x \neq 0$, then choose s and e so that

$$(20.2) \qquad |x| = s \times \beta^e, \quad \text{where} \quad \beta^{-1}(1 - \tfrac{1}{2}\beta^{-t}) \leq s < 1 - \tfrac{1}{2}\beta^{-t}.$$

If e is outside the interval $-m \leq e \leq M$, we have no reasonable possibility of representing x well with the available exponents; here we shall only say that x is outside the range of floating-point numbers and shall not proceed further. If e is within the interval, we take the infinite base-β expansion of $s + \tfrac{1}{2}\beta^{-t}$ (the one ending with zeroes if there is a choice) and chop off all digits after the first t to the right of the radical point. Then x_R consists of the sign of x, the t digits just obtained, and the e obtained in (20.2).

(20.3) **Exercise.** If $\beta^{e-1}(1 - \tfrac{1}{2}\beta^{-t}) \leq |x| < \beta^e(1 - \tfrac{1}{2}\beta^{-t})$, show that

$$x_R = \text{sign}(x) \cdot \text{entier}(\beta^{t-e}|x| + \tfrac{1}{2}) \cdot \beta^{e-t},$$

where entier (y) denotes the greatest integer not exceeding y. (Mathematicians also use the notations $[y]$ and $E(y)$ for the same function.)

The following theorem is the most fundamental in floating-point rounding-error theory; it gives a convenient expression for the relative error committed if one replaces x by x_R.

(20.4) **Theorem.** *If x is a real number within the range of floating-point numbers, then*

$$(20.5) \qquad x_R = x(1 + \delta), \quad \text{where} \quad |\delta| \leq \tfrac{1}{2}\beta^{1-t}.$$

To prove (20.4), assume $x > 0$ since the case $x < 0$ can be handled analogously and the case $x = x_R = 0$ is trivial. Let e be the unique integer for which

$$\beta^{e-1} \leq x < \beta^e.$$

In the interval $[\beta^{e-1}, \beta^e]$ the floating-point numbers are uniformly spaced with a separation of β^{e-t}. The closest one to x is x_R and it must be within a distance of $\tfrac{1}{2}\beta^{e-t}$ from x. That is,

$$|x_R - x| \leq \tfrac{1}{2}\beta^{e-t}.$$

Since $\beta^{e-1} \leq x$, we have

$$\frac{|x_R - x|}{|x|} \leq \frac{\frac{1}{2}\beta^{e-t}}{\beta^{e-1}} = \frac{1}{2}\beta^{1-t}.$$

Finally, since

$$\delta = (x_R - x)/x,$$

we have proved the theorem.

As an example, let $\beta = 10$, $t = 4$, and $x = \pi$. The decimal representation of π begins

$$3.14159265\cdots = +.314159265\cdots \times 10^1.$$

Thus $e = 1$ and $x_R = .3142 \times 10^1$. Hence

$$\delta = (x_R - x)/x = -.00012966\cdots.$$

Since $\frac{1}{2}\beta^{1-t} = \frac{1}{2}(10^{-3}) = 0.0005$, we see that δ easily satisfies $|\delta| \leq \frac{1}{2}\beta^{1-t}$.

To show that $\frac{1}{2}\beta^{1-t}$ is almost the best possible bound for $|\delta|$, consider $x = \beta^a(1 + \frac{1}{2}\beta^{1-t})$ for some a. Then

$$\frac{|x_R - x|}{|x|} = \frac{\frac{1}{2}\beta^{1-t} \cdot \beta^a}{\beta^a(1 + \frac{1}{2}\beta^{1-t})} = \frac{\frac{1}{2}\beta^{1-t}}{1 + \frac{1}{2}\beta^{1-t}},$$

which is very close to $\frac{1}{2}\beta^{1-t}$ for practical values of t.

A second way of representing real numbers by floating-point numbers is *chopping*. Given a real number in the range of floating-point numbers, we pick x_C ("x chopped") as the unique number in F which is closest to x under the constraint $|x_C| \leq |x|$. One can obtain x_C by taking the infinite base-β expansion of x (the one ending with zeroes if there is a choice) and chopping off the significant digits after the t most significant ones.

(20.6) **Exercise.** If $\beta^{a-1} \leq |x| < \beta^a$, prove that

$$x_C = \text{sign}(x) \cdot \text{entier}(\beta^{t-a}|x|)\beta^{a-t}.$$

(20.7) **Exercise.** If x is within the range of floating-point numbers, prove that

$$x_C = x(1 + \delta), \quad \text{where} \quad |\delta| < \beta^{1-t}.$$

Next we wish to discuss the rounding errors in arithmetic operations. We cannot consider all machines at once for there is wide variation in their operations. However, the error bounds on different machines do not vary greatly. We shall confine ourselves to two kinds of arithmetic—*rounded* and *chopped* operations.

Given two floating-point numbers x, y, we shall denote by

$$\text{fl}\,(x + y), \quad \text{fl}\,(x - y), \quad \text{fl}\,(x \times y), \quad \text{fl}\,(x/y)$$

the results of floating-point addition, subtraction, multiplication, and division, respectively, whether the result is rounded or chopped. We shall assume that the floating-point system behaves as follows:

Rounded operation: For any two numbers x, y in F, the exact real number $x + y$, $x - y$, $x \times y$, or x/y is obtained and then rounded. (We assume $y \neq 0$ for division.) Thus

$$\text{fl}\,(x + y) = (x + y)_R; \quad \text{fl}\,(x - y) = (x - y)_R;$$
$$\text{fl}\,(x \times y) = (xy)_R; \quad \text{fl}\,(x/y) = (x/y)_R.$$

Chopped operation: For any two numbers x, y in F, we have

$$\text{fl}\,(x \pm y) = (x \pm y)_C; \quad \text{fl}\,(x \times y) = (xy)_C; \quad \text{fl}\,(x/y) = (x/y)_C.$$

From (20.4) and (20.7) we then have the following theorem:

(20.8)   **Theorem.**   *Let $*$ denote any of the operators $+, -, \times, /$. Then*

$$\text{fl}\,(x * y) = (x * y)(1 + \delta),$$

where
$$\begin{cases} |\delta| \leq \tfrac{1}{2}\beta^{1-t} & \textit{(rounded operations)} \\ |\delta| < \beta^{1-t} & \textit{(chopped operations)}. \end{cases}$$

In most cases rounded operations are preferable to chopped ones. For one thing, the error bound is half as large for rounded operations. A more important consideration is the following: In adding a large number n of positive numbers with chopped arithmetic, each chopping error is of the same sign and the bias thereby introduced can result in a very substantial error after n steps. In rounded arithmetic, the errors will ordinarily be positive and negative and the cancellation of the errors of different sign will normally reduce the total error after n terms to a much smaller magnitude than that which would result from chopped operations. In fact, if the errors all have the same magnitude and if their signs are independent and equally likely to be $+$ or $-$, the central-limit theorem of probability tells us that a typical error after a chopped sum of n positive terms will probably be roughly $\sqrt{n}$ times as large as the error from a rounded sum.

In spite of these considerations, chopped arithmetic is surprisingly common in floating-point systems and will be found, for example, in FORTRAN

II and FORTRAN IV for the 7090 computer. In very delicate computations, there are occasional advantages in chopped arithmetic because the sign of the chopping error is known.

Because of its frequent occurrence in error bounds (see above), we introduce the following abbreviation:

(20.9) **Definition.** Let u stand for a *unit round-off*, measured in relative terms. Thus

$$\begin{cases} u = \tfrac{1}{2}\beta^{1-t} & \text{(rounded operations)} \\ u = \beta^{1-t} & \text{(chopped operations).} \end{cases}$$

From the above fundamental bounds for floating operations, we can build others. For example, if we define fl $(x + y + z)$ to mean

$$\text{fl (fl } (x + y) + z),$$

we have

$$\begin{aligned} \text{fl } (x + y + z) &= \text{fl } ((x + y)(1 + \delta_1) + z) \\ &= ((x + y)(1 + \delta_1) + z)(1 + \delta_2) \\ &= (x + y)(1 + \delta_1)(1 + \delta_2) + z(1 + \delta_2), \quad |\delta_i| \le u. \end{aligned}$$

(20.10)

In the same way, if we assume the addition of terms in order from $i = 1$ to $i = 4$, we have

$$\text{fl } (x_i \times y_i) = x_i y_i (1 + \delta_i), \quad |\delta_i| \le u,$$

so that

$$\text{fl }\left(\sum_{i=1}^{4} x_i \times y_i \right) = (((x_1 y_1(1 + \delta_1) + x_2 y_2(1 + \delta_2))(1 + \delta_5)$$

$$+ x_3 y_3(1 + \delta_3))(1 + \delta_6) + x_4 y_4(1 + \delta_4))(1 + \delta_7)$$

(20.11)

$$= x_1 y_1(1 + \delta_1)(1 + \delta_5)(1 + \delta_6)(1 + \delta_7)$$

$$+ x_2 y_2(1 + \delta_2)(1 + \delta_5)(1 + \delta_6)(1 + \delta_7)$$

$$+ x_3 y_3(1 + \delta_3)(1 + \delta_6)(1 + \delta_7)$$

$$+ x_4 y_4(1 + \delta_4)(1 + \delta_7),$$

where $|\delta_i| \le u$ for all i.

Because the products of $1 + \delta_i$ appear so often, it is desirable to obtain some usable bounds for them. The following lemmas will help.

(20.12) **Lemma.** *If* $0 \le u < 1$, *and if* $n = 1, 2, 3, \ldots$, *then*

$$1 - nu \le (1 - u)^n.$$

Proof: Let $f(u) = (1 - u)^n$. Then by Taylor's theorem,

$$f(u) = f(0) + uf'(0) + \frac{f''(\theta u)}{2} u^2, \quad 0 < \theta < 1$$

$$= 1 - nu + \frac{n(n - 1)}{2} (1 - \theta u)^{n-2} u^2.$$

Since the remainder term is nonnegative, we have $f(u) \geq 1 - nu$, proving (20.12).

(20.13) **Lemma.** *If $n = 1, 2, \ldots,$ and if $0 \leq nu \leq .01$, then*

$$(1 + u)^n \leq 1 + 1.01nu.$$

Proof: It can be shown that

(20.14) $$1 + x \leq e^x \quad \text{for all} \quad x \geq 0;$$

(20.15) $$e^x \leq 1 + 1.01x \quad \text{for} \quad 0 \leq x \leq .01.$$

(We leave proofs of these inequalities to the reader.) Then

$$(1 + u)^n \leq (e^u)^n = e^{nu}, \quad \text{by (20.14)}$$

$$\leq 1 + 1.01nu, \quad \text{by (20.15)}.$$

In the applications that we have in mind for this lemma, n is the order of a matrix and u is the unit round-off. Hence the hypothesis $nu \leq 0.01$ is certainly satisfied in any practical problems.

(20.16) **Lemma.** *If $|\delta_i| \leq u$ for $i = 1, \ldots, n$, and if $nu \leq 0.01$, then*

(20.17) $$1 - nu \leq \prod_1^n (1 + \delta_i) \leq 1 + 1.01nu.$$

Proof: Since

$$(1 - u)^n \leq \prod_1^n (1 + \delta_i) \leq (1 + u)^n,$$

the proof follows from (20.12) and (20.13).

Note: It is convenient to rewrite (20.17) in the form

$$\prod_1^n (1 + \delta_i) = 1 + 1.01n\theta u, \quad |\theta| \leq 1.$$

Using (20.16), we can rewrite the earlier result (20.11) as follows if $4u \leq 0.01$:

$$\mathrm{fl}\left(\sum_{i=1}^{4} x_i \times y_i\right) = x_1 y_1(1 + 4.04\theta_1 u) + x_2 y_2(1 + 4.04\theta_2 u)$$
$$+ x_3 y_3(1 + 3.03\theta_3 u) + x_4 y_4(1 + 2.02\theta_4 u), \quad |\theta_i| \leq 1.$$

Similarly, we can prove the following theorem:

(20.18)   **Theorem.**   *If $nu \leq 0.01$, then*

$$(20.19) \qquad \mathrm{fl}\left(\sum_{i=1}^{n} x_i \times y_i\right) = \sum_{i=1}^{n} x_i y_i [1 + 1.01(n + 2 - i)\theta_i u], \quad |\theta_i| \leq 1.$$

In stating (20.19) we have increased the bound for $i = 1$ from $1.01n\theta_1 u$ to $1.01(n + 1)\theta_1 u$ for simplicity.

These floating-point bounds enable us to estimate the error in quite extensive computations. One of the commonest operations in matrix computation is forming the inner product of two vectors. For example, the inner product of vectors x and y is $\sum_{i=1}^{n} x_i y_i$. This operation would occur n^2 times in multiplying two matrices together. Some digital computers (e.g., most desk calculators) have the facility to accumulate an inner product in a register without having to store the intermediate totals $\sum_{i=1}^{k} x_i y_i$. This is an advantage in eliminating some store and fetch operations and also in using index registers efficiently on some computers. (Such advantages were basic factors in the development of the Crout algorithm.) Also there can be a large reduction in the rounding error in matrix operations if the accumulation register (as in a desk calculator) has appreciably more digits in its significand than the number of digits of x_i and y_i. Since there are many times when the rounding error must be reduced to a minimum, we give the relevant bounds for this double-precision accumulation. They can be compared with the bounds for single-precision accumulation given by (20.19).

To be explicit, suppose that x_i and y_i are all stored as ordinary floating-point numbers with t digits in each significand but that the accumulating total is carried in a floating-point register with $2t$ digits in its significand. After the complete inner product has been accumulated, it is rounded to t digits and stored. We denote the rounded t-digit answer by

$$\mathrm{fl}_2\left(\sum_{i=1}^{n} x_i \times y_i\right).$$

How can we represent the rounding error in the computed inner product?
Up to the time of the final rounding to t digits, the accumulating inner
product behaves approximately like ordinary floating-point arithmetic with
$2t$ digits, except that there is no error in multiplication. If it behaved in
exactly this way, then from (20.19) the double-precision accumulated inner
product could be represented by

$$(20.20) \qquad \sum_{i=1}^{n} x_i y_i \{1 + 1.01(n + 1 - i)\theta_i F \tfrac{1}{2}\beta^{1-2t}\}, \quad |\theta_i| \leq 1,$$

with $F = 1$. However, the addition of double-precision numbers is usually
done with more relative error than single-precision addition, and so the
representation (20.20) is not normally provable. Without explanation or
proof, we state that the representation (20.20) holds for typical double-
precision accumulation with the factor $F = 1 + 1/\beta$. See Wilkinson (1963)
for a detailed explanation when $\beta = 2$ or 10.

As far as the principal result (20.21) is concerned, the difference between
$F = 1$ and $1 + 1/\beta$ is practically immaterial. Because of the final rounding
to t digits, we have

(20.21)

$$\mathrm{fl}_2\left(\sum_{i=1}^{n} x_i \times y_i\right) = (1 + \theta_0 \tfrac{1}{2}\beta^{1-t}) \sum_{i=1}^{n} x_i y_i \{1 + 1.01(n + 1 - i)\theta_i F \tfrac{1}{2}\beta^{1-2t}\},$$

where $F = 1 + 1/\beta$ and all $|\theta_i| \leq 1$. On practical machines, for achievable
values of n the value of $1.01 n F \tfrac{1}{2}\beta^{1-2t}$ is less than $u = \tfrac{1}{2}\beta^{1-t}$ by many orders of
magnitude. Unless there is great cancellation, (20.21) states that

$$\mathrm{fl}_2\left(\sum_{i=1}^{n} x_i \times y_i\right)$$

differs from the true $\sum_{i=1}^{n} x_i y_i$ by negligibly more than a single round-off error.

(20.22) **Exercise.** Show by means of an example with $\beta = 10$, $t = 3$ that
$\mathrm{fl}_2\left(\sum_{i=1}^{n} x_i \times y_i\right)$ can differ from $\sum_{i=1}^{n} x_i y_i$ by a large relative amount
when there is cancellation.

(20.23) **Exercise.** Prove from (20.21) that if nu is sufficiently small

$$\left| \mathrm{fl}_2\left(\sum_{i=1}^{n} x_i \times y_i\right) - \sum_{i=1}^{n} x_i y_i \right| \leq 1.01u \cdot \|x\|_2 \cdot \|y\|_2.$$

An instructive way to look at all the above error estimates is that they express the results of a floating-point computation as the results of exact arithmetic operations on slightly perturbed operands or data. Thus

$$\text{fl}\,(x \times y) = xy(1 + \delta)$$

can be interpreted as the exact product of two unknown numbers $x' = x$ and $y' = y(1 + \delta)$ which differ relatively little from x and y, respectively. Or, as one of many alternatives, we could have defined $x' = x(1 + \delta)^{1/2}$ and $y' = y(1 + \delta)^{1/2}$. This point of view is called *inverse round-off analysis* since the errors are referred back to the data.

In *direct round-off analysis* one regards floating multiplication (for example) as an operation which approximates true multiplication. One then gives bounds for the difference between the floating product $\text{fl}\,(x \times y)$ and the true product xy. The difficulty here is that floating multiplication is not an associative operation, and hence ordinary analysis cannot be used with it. An entirely new system of analysis must be devised, and it is very cumbersome and tedious. (See, for example, Chap. 1 of Householder (1953).) Moreover, floating addition is not associative, and the distributive laws also fail.

Since in inverse round-off analysis the result of a floating-point operation is interpreted as the result of ordinary real arithmetic, we may use the rules of algebra without difficulty. This method is therefore easier to use and less susceptible to human blunders.

Inverse round-off analysis was introduced by Givens (1954) in a monumental paper. In other areas of error theory the inverse idea had been used earlier by Lanczos (his τ-method) and has been published, for example, in Lanczos (1956).

Sometimes an inverse error analysis can be an end in itself, as in these two examples. First, suppose that one is interested in solving a linear system $Ax = b$. The inverse error analysis given in Sec. 21 will state that the computed answer x is precisely the solution of a linear system $A'x = b$, where A' is a certain unknown matrix with the property that $\|A' - A\| < \epsilon$, some stated small number. Now if we know in advance that A is itself undetermined or subject to an error which is much larger than ϵ, we should be satisfied that the computed x is as good an answer as we are entitled to get. It would seem hardly necessary to ask how close x is to the "true" answer $A^{-1}b$.

As a second example, we ask the reader to imagine that the vector x represents the position of a rocket at a large number of times on a trip from Earth to Mars. Suppose also that Ax represents the time derivative of the momentum of the rocket at the same set of times. Finally, suppose that b represents the net force on the rocket at the same times, including both the external forces and those of the rocket's own propulsion. Then the equation system $Ax = b$ represents the balance of actual and inertial forces. For any given b, a true solution x represents a trajectory. We can also say that a computed x exactly satisfies a system $Ax = b + \delta b$. In other words, the rocket could be kept on the trajectory x by the application of additional forces δb. If we know that $\|\delta b\| < \epsilon$, we have a bound for the magnitude of the necessary corrective forces. If ϵ is safely less than the magnitude of corrective forces available to the rocket in the form of reserve thrust, we can be sure that the computed trajectory x can be achieved. That is, any rounding error we might have made in computing x can be easily compensated for by an available change of b. It may thus be more useful to examine the magnitude of δb than to ask how wrong x is for a fixed right member b.

Despite the above two examples, there are many times when the proposer of a physical problem really wants to know how close a computed solution x of the system $Ax = b$ is to the true solution $A^{-1}b$. Again, inverse error analysis can be a very useful intermediate step in answering the question. For, once we know that $Ax = b + \delta b$, where $\|\delta b\| < \epsilon$, we know that

$$\begin{aligned}
\|x - A^{-1}b\| &= \|A^{-1}(Ax - b)\| \\
&= \|A^{-1}(\delta b)\| \\
&\le \|A^{-1}\| \cdot \|\delta b\| \\
&< \|A^{-1}\| \cdot \epsilon.
\end{aligned}$$

Hence, if we have some upper bound for $\|A^{-1}\|$, we can convert a bound on $\|\delta b\|$ into a bound on $\|x - A^{-1}b\|$. This approach to bounding $\|x - A^{-1}b\|$ can be much easier than a frontal attack via direct round-off analysis.

(20.24) **Exercise.**   Let $Q(t)$ be the result of computing the value of the polynomial

$$P(t) = \sum_{k=0}^{n} a_k t^k$$

by the following algorithm:

$q := a_n;$

   for $k := n - 1$ **step** -1 **until** 0 **do**

   $q := \mathrm{fl}\,(t \times q + a_k).$

Prove that

$$Q(t) = \sum_{k=0}^{n} [1 + 1.01(2k + 1)\theta_k u] a_k t^k,$$

where all $|\theta_k| \le 1$. (Assume that t, the a_k, and all intermediate answers are floating-point numbers.)

(20.25) **Research problem.** Investigate the rounding error in using (14.2) as a method of avoiding exponent over- and underflow in evaluating det (A). Consider two situations: when double-precision logarithms are and are not available.

(20.26) **Exercise.** Prove (20.14) and (20.15).

(20.27) **Exercise.** In some applications, as W. Kahan has shown, another version of theorem (20.8) leads to slightly simpler expressions: Prove

(20.28) **Theorem.** *Let* $*$ *denote any of the operators* $+$, $-$, $\times$, $/$. *Then*

$$\mathrm{fl}\,(x * y) = \frac{x * y}{1 + \delta},$$

$$where \begin{cases} |\delta| \leq \tfrac{1}{2}\beta^{1-t} & (rounded\ operations) \\ |\delta| < \beta^{1-t} & (chopped\ operations). \end{cases}$$

21. ROUNDING ERROR IN GAUSSIAN ELIMINATION

In the next two sections we shall combine the tools introduced in the previous sections—vector and matrix norms, Gaussian elimination, iterative improvement, and floating-point rounding-error analysis—to study the detailed behavior of our algorithms on a computer.

Let A, b, and x be the given matrix, the given right-hand side, and the solution computed by Gaussian elimination with pivoting, respectively. (The elements of A, b, and x must be floating-point numbers.) In this section we show that the computed solution x exactly satisfies a perturbed equation

$$(21.1) \qquad (A + \delta A)x = b,$$

where δA is a certain "small" matrix, and we give an upper bound for the smallness of δA in terms of A and the unit round-off u. Note that the expression (21.1) is an example of an inverse-error expression, as just described in Sec. 20.

Most of the ideas we shall use have been developed over the last several years by J. H. Wilkinson (1961), (1963), (1965). We have simply adapted his work to our particular situation. See also Fox (1964) and Wendroff (1966).

We find it convenient to use the *maximum norms* for vectors and matrices rather than the euclidean norms used earlier. These norms, mentioned also in Secs. 2 and 11, are defined by

$$(21.2) \qquad \|x\|_\infty = \max_{1 \le i \le n} |x_i|,$$

if $x = (x_1, \ldots, x_n)^T$ is a vector; and by

$$(21.3) \qquad \|A\|_\infty = \max_{1 \le i \le n} \sum_{j=1}^{n} |a_{i,j}|,$$

if $A = (a_{i,j})$ is a matrix. It is easy to see that if x is a vector satisfying $|x_i| \le c$, $i = 1, \ldots, n$, then

$$(21.4) \qquad \|x\|_\infty \le c;$$

and, if A and B are matrices with $|a_{i,j}| \le |b_{i,j}|$, $i, j = 1, \ldots, n$, then

$$(21.5) \qquad \|A\|_\infty \le \|B\|_\infty.$$

The euclidean norm (2.6) fails to possess property (21.5).

The reader will recall from exercise (2.18) that

$$(21.6) \qquad \|A\|_\infty = \max_{\|x\|_\infty = 1} \|Ax\|_\infty.$$

As we have seen, the first and biggest step in Gaussian elimination is the decomposition of the matrix A into the product of two triangular matrices L and U. We assume that A is initially given with its rows scaled and ordered in such a way that no pivoting is needed. In practice, of course, this may not be true. But pivoting only involves permutations of the row subscripts and is irrelevant to the error analysis; so we will simply neglect it in our notation.

The decomposition consists of computing a sequence of matrices $A^{(1)} = A, A^{(2)}, \ldots, A^{(n)}$, where the matrix $A^{(k)}$ is zero below the diagonal in the first $k - 1$ columns. The matrix $A^{(k+1)}$ is obtained from $A^{(k)}$ by subtracting a multiple of the k-th row from each of the rows below it; the rest of $A^{(k)}$ is left unchanged. The multipliers are chosen so that if there were no rounding errors $A^{(k+1)}$ would have zeros below the diagonal in the k-th column. We do not calculate these elements but take them to be zero by definition. (In our programs these "holes" in A are used to store the multipliers, but this does not affect this error analysis.)

More precisely, let $A^{(k)}$ have elements $a_{i,j}^{(k)}$. Then let

(21.7) $$m_{i,k} = \text{fl} \, (a_{i,k}^{(k)}/a_{k,k}^{(k)}), \quad i \geq k + 1,$$

and

(21.8) $$a_{i,j}^{(k+1)} = \begin{cases} 0, & \text{for } i \geq k+1, \ j = k \\ \text{fl} \, (a_{i,j}^{(k)} - m_{i,k} \times a_{k,j}^{(k)}), & \text{for } i \geq k+1, \ j \geq k+1 \\ a_{i,j}^{(k)}, & \text{otherwise.} \end{cases}$$

Fig. (21.9) illustrates the portions of the matrix involved in the three different cases. These steps are carried out for $k = 1, \ldots, n - 1$.

(21.9)

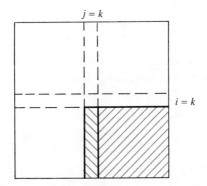

Finally, let

$$(21.10) \qquad\qquad U = A^{(n)}$$

and

$$(21.11) \qquad L = \begin{bmatrix} 1 & & & & & \\ m_{2,1} & 1 & & & \bigcirc & \\ m_{3,1} & m_{3,2} & & & & \\ \cdot & \cdot & \cdot & & & \\ \cdot & \cdot & & \cdot & & \\ \cdot & \cdot & & & \cdot & \\ m_{n,1} & m_{n,2} & \cdot & \cdot & \cdot & 1 \end{bmatrix}$$

Clearly L and U are lower and upper triangular, respectively. We want to prove that

$$LU = A + E,$$

where E is a matrix of small elements which account for the rounding errors.

The error in the calculation of the multiplier $m_{i,k}$ is expressed by

$$(21.12) \qquad m_{i,k} = (a_{i,k}^{(k)}/a_{k,k}^{(k)})(1 + \delta_{i,k}), \quad \text{where} \quad |\delta_{i,k}| \le u,$$

or

$$(21.13) \qquad\qquad 0 = a_{i,k}^{(k)} - m_{i,k}a_{k,k}^{(k)} + a_{i,k}^{(k)}\delta_{i,k}.$$

That is,

$$(21.14) \qquad\qquad \epsilon_{i,k}^{(k)} = a_{i,k}^{(k)}\delta_{i,k}, \quad \text{for} \quad i \ge k + 1$$

is the error made by setting $a_{i,k}^{(k+1)}$ equal to 0. For the second case of (21.8) we have (using both (20.8) and (20.28))

$$a_{i,j}^{(k+1)} = \text{fl}\,(a_{i,j}^{(k)} - \text{fl}\,(m_{i,k} \times a_{k,j}^{(k)}))$$

$$(21.15) \qquad\quad = (a_{i,j}^{(k)} - m_{i,k}a_{k,j}^{(k)}(1 + \delta_{i,j}))/(1 + \delta_{i,j}'), \quad \text{where} \quad |\delta_{i,j}| \le u$$

$$\text{and} \quad |\delta_{i,j}'| \le u,$$

or

$$(21.16) \qquad a_{i,j}^{(k+1)} = a_{i,j}^{(k)} - m_{i,k}a_{k,j}^{(k)} - m_{i,k}a_{k,j}^{(k)}\delta_{i,j} - a_{i,j}^{(k+1)}\delta_{i,j}'.$$

That is,

$$(21.17) \quad \epsilon_{i,j}^{(k)} = -m_{i,k}a_{k,j}^{(k)}\delta_{i,j} - a_{i,j}^{(k+1)}\delta_{i,j}' \quad (\text{for} \quad i \geq k+1, \quad j \geq k+1)$$

is the error in the calculation of the $a_{i,j}^{(k+1)}$ for the "new" part of $A^{(k+1)}$. The rest of $A^{(k+1)}$ is taken directly from $A^{(k)}$, so there is no error.

In summary,

$$(21.18) \quad \epsilon_{i,j}^{(k)} = \begin{cases} a_{i,k}^{(k)}\delta_{i,k}, & \text{for} \quad i \geq k+1, \quad j = k \\ -m_{i,k}a_{k,j}^{(k)}\delta_{i,j} - a_{i,j}^{(k+1)}\delta_{i,j}', & \text{for} \quad i \geq k+1, \quad j \geq k+1 \\ 0, & \text{otherwise.} \end{cases}$$

Thus, if we let $E^{(k)}$ be the matrix with elements $\epsilon_{i,j}^{(k)}$ and let

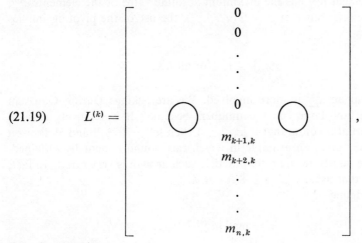

$$(21.19) \qquad L^{(k)} = \begin{bmatrix} & & 0 & & \\ & & 0 & & \\ & & \cdot & & \\ & & \cdot & & \\ & & \cdot & & \\ & & 0 & & \\ & \bigcirc & & \bigcirc & \\ & & m_{k+1,k} & & \\ & & m_{k+2,k} & & \\ & & \cdot & & \\ & & \cdot & & \\ & & \cdot & & \\ & & m_{n,k} & & \end{bmatrix},$$

then the equation

$$(21.20) \qquad\qquad A^{(k+1)} = A^{(k)} - L^{(k)}A^{(k)} + E^{(k)}$$

completely describes one step of the decomposition, including the rounding error. Adding these equations for $k = 1, \ldots, n-1$, we have

$$L^{(1)}A^{(1)} + L^{(2)}A^{(2)} + \cdots + L^{(n-1)}A^{(n-1)} + A^{(n)}$$
$$= A^{(1)} + E^{(1)} + E^{(2)} + \cdots + E^{(n-1)}.$$

The matrix $L^{(k)}A^{(k)}$ depends upon only the k-th row of $A^{(k)}$, and this row is equal to the k-th row of $A^{(n)}$. Thus we have

$$(L^{(1)} + \cdots + L^{(n-1)} + I)A^{(n)} = A^{(1)} + E^{(1)} + \cdots + E^{(n-1)}.$$

That is,

$$(21.21) \qquad\qquad LU = A + E,$$

where L and U are defined by (21.10) and (21.11) and where

$$(21.22) \qquad\qquad E = E^{(1)} + E^{(2)} + \cdots + E^{(n-1)}$$

is the sum of the errors at the individual steps. We have achieved the first objective: proving (21.21).

Our next task is to bound the size of E. For this we need bounds on the numbers $m_{i,k}$ and $a_{i,j}^{(k)}$, which appear in the $\epsilon_{i,j}^{(k)}$. Pivoting is used just to keep these bounds small. We have assumed that the rows of A are ordered so that the pivot element $a_{k,k}^{(k)}$ has the maximum absolute value of the elements $a_{i,k}^{(k)}$, for $i = k, \ldots, n$. Since $m_{i,k} = \text{fl}\,(a_{i,k}^{(k)}/a_{k,k}^{(k)})$, the use of the pivoting implies that

$$(21.23) \qquad\qquad |m_{i,k}| \leq 1, \quad \text{for all } i, k.$$

A bound on $a_{i,j}^{(k)}$ is more involved. We are asking: During Gaussian elimination, how large can the numbers become? It is relatively easy to show for partial pivoting that if $|a_{i,j}| \leq 1$ then $|a_{i,j}^{(k)}| \leq 2^{k-1}$, and Wilkinson (1961), (1963) gives an example in which this bound is actually obtained. However, he points out that "in practice, such growth is very rare." In fact, he observes that usually $|a_{i,j}^{(k)}| \leq 8$ for all k.

Let us define

$$(21.24) \qquad\qquad \rho = \max_{i,j,k} |a_{i,j}^{(k)}|/\|A\|_\infty.$$

Although we have no good a priori bound for ρ, it could be computed relatively easily for any given matrix during the course of the triangular decomposition. With this definition we have

$$|a_{i,j}^{(k)}| \leq \rho \, \|A\|_\infty.$$

This, together with (21.18) and (21.23), gives

$$(21.25) \qquad |\epsilon_{i,j}^{(k)}| \leq \rho \, \|A\|_\infty \cdot \begin{cases} u, & \text{for } i \geq k+1, \; j = k \\ 2u, & \text{for } i \geq k+1, \; j \geq k+1 \\ 0, & \text{otherwise.} \end{cases}$$

Following (21.22), we add the $\epsilon_{i,j}^{(k)}$ together to get E. Then

$$(21.26) \quad |E| \leq \rho \, \|A\|_\infty \, u \begin{bmatrix} 0 & 0 & 0 & \cdot & \cdot & \cdot & 0 & 0 \\ 1 & 2 & 2 & \cdot & \cdot & \cdot & 2 & 2 \\ 1 & 3 & 4 & \cdot & \cdot & \cdot & 4 & 4 \\ & \cdot & \cdot & \cdot & & & \cdot & \cdot & \cdot \\ 1 & 3 & 5 & \cdot & \cdot & \cdot & 2n-4 & 2n-4 \\ 1 & 3 & 5 & \cdot & \cdot & \cdot & 2n-3 & 2n-2 \end{bmatrix},$$

where the inequality holds element by element. The matrix on the right-hand side can easily be reconstructed because its elements are simply the number of arithmetic operations necessary to compute the corresponding entry in the LU tableau.

Finally, using definition (21.3) for $\|E\|_\infty$ we find that

$$\|E\|_\infty \leq \rho \, \|A\|_\infty \left(\sum_{j=1}^{n} (2j-1) - 1 \right) u \leq n^2 \rho \, \|A\|_\infty \, u.$$

This, then, is one of the principal results of this section:

(21.27) **Theorem.** *The matrices L and U computed by Gaussian elimination with pivoting, using floating-point arithmetic with unit round-off u, satisfy*

$$LU = A + E,$$

with

$$(21.28) \qquad\qquad \|E\|_\infty \leq n^2 \rho \, \|A\|_\infty \, u.$$

In other words L and U form the *exact* decomposition of some slightly perturbed matrix. Unless ρ is very large, the perturbations are of the order of rounding errors in the elements of A.

Once we have L and U, we find the solution to $Ax = b$ by successively solving the two triangular systems $Ly = b$ and $Ux = y$. We therefore wish to bound the rounding errors introduced in solving a general triangular system—for example,

$$Rx = b.$$

If R is lower triangular we compute the components of x in the order x_1, $x_2, \ldots, x_n$ by

(21.29)
$$x_1 := \text{fl}\,(b_1/r_{1,1})$$
$$x_i := \text{fl}\left(\frac{-r_{i,1}x_1 - r_{i,2}x_2 - \cdots - r_{i,i-1}x_{i-1} + b_i}{r_{i,i}}\right), \quad i = 2, \ldots, n.$$

We could use accumulated inner products and obtain a very accurate answer. But, since we already have some error in L and U, the extra computer time does not seem justified. So, slightly extending theorem (20.18) for the round-off error in an ordinary inner product, we see that

(21.30)
$$x_1 = \frac{b_1}{r_{1,1}(1 + \delta_{1,1})}$$
$$x_i = \frac{-r_{i,1}(1 + \delta_{i,1})x_1 - \cdots - r_{i,i-1}(1 + \delta_{i,i-1})x_{i-1} + b_i}{r_{i,i}(1 + \delta_{i,i})(1 + \delta'_{i,i})},$$
$$(i = 2, \ldots, n),$$

with

(21.31)
$$|\delta_{i,i}| \le u, \quad |\delta'_{i,i}| \le u, \qquad i = 1, \ldots, n$$
$$|\delta_{i,1}| \le (i - 1) \cdot 1.01u, \qquad i = 2, \ldots, n$$
$$|\delta_{i,j}| \le (i + 1 - j) \cdot 1.01u, \quad i = 2, \ldots, n, \quad j = 2, \ldots, i - 1.$$

Note that both (20.8) and (20.28) are used in such a way that all the factors $1 + \delta$ multiply elements of R.

(21.32) **Exercise.** Supply the details in the proof of (21.30) and (21.31).

The equations (21.30) can be written in the form

(21.33)
$$r_{1,1}(1 + \delta_{1,1})x_1 = b_1$$
$$r_{i,1}(1 + \delta_{i,1})x_1 + \cdots + r_{i,i}(1 + \delta_{i,i})(1 + \delta'_{i,i})x_i = b_i,$$
$$i = 2, \ldots, n,$$

or

(21.34)
$$(R + \delta R)x = b,$$

where

(21.35)

$$
|\delta R| \leq 1.01u
\begin{bmatrix}
|r_{1,1}| \\[2ex]
|r_{2,1}| & 2\,|r_{2,2}| \\[2ex]
2\,|r_{3,1}| & 2\,|r_{3,2}| & 2\,|r_{3,3}| \\[2ex]
3\,|r_{4,1}| & 3|r_{4,2}| & 2\,|r_{4,3}| & 2|r_{4,4}| \\[2ex]
\cdot & \cdot & \cdot & \cdot\ \cdot \\[1ex]
\cdot & \cdot & \cdot & \cdot\ \ \cdot \\[1ex]
\cdot & \cdot & \cdot & \cdot\ \ \ \cdot \\[1ex]
(n-1)\,|r_{n,1}| & (n-1)\,|r_{n,2}| & (n-2)\,|r_{n,3}| & (n-3)\,|r_{n,4}| \cdots 2\,|r_{n,n}|
\end{bmatrix}
.
$$

Consequently,

(21.36) $$\|\delta R\|_\infty \leq \frac{n(n+1)}{2} \cdot 1.01u \cdot \max_{i,j} |r_{i,j}| .$$

To summarize:

(21.37)   **Theorem.** *The vector x computed by* (21.29) *is the exact solution of a perturbed triangular system* $(R + \delta R)x = b$, *where the perturbation* δR *satisfies* (21.35) *and* (21.36).

Again, the perturbations are of the order of rounding errors. However, by comparing (21.35) with (21.26) we see that the individual elements of δR are proportional to the corresponding elements of R, but that the elements of E are not so directly related to those of A.

Applying (21.37) to the two triangular systems $Ly = b$ and $Ux = y$, we find that the final computed x satisfies

$$(L + \delta L)(U + \delta U)x = b$$

or, since $LU = A + E$,

(21.38) $$(A + E + (\delta L)U + L\,\delta U + \delta L\,\delta U)x = b.$$

The matrices L and U satisfy

$$|l_{i,j}| \leq 1,$$
$$|u_{i,j}| \leq \rho\,\|A\|_{\infty},$$

where ρ is given by (21.24). Hence

(21.39) $$\left\{ \begin{array}{l} \|L\|_{\infty} \leq n, \\[2mm] \|U\|_{\infty} \leq n\rho\,\|A\|_{\infty}; \\[2mm] \|\delta L\|_{\infty} \leq \dfrac{n(n+1)}{2} \cdot 1.01u, \\[3mm] \|\delta U\|_{\infty} \leq \dfrac{n(n+1)}{2} \cdot 1.01\rho\,\|A\|_{\infty}\,u. \end{array} \right.$$

Remember from (21.27) that

$$\|E\|_{\infty} \leq n^2\rho\,\|A\|_{\infty}\,u.$$

Since $n^2 u \ll 1$ in any contemplated application, we may write

$$\|\delta L\|_{\infty} \cdot \|\delta U\|_{\infty} \leq n^2\rho\,\|A\|_{\infty}\,u.$$

Finally, if we let

(21.40) $$\delta A = E + (\delta L)U + L\,\delta U + \delta L\,\delta U$$

then $\|\delta A\|_{\infty} \leq \|E\|_{\infty} + \|\delta L\|_{\infty} \cdot \|U\|_{\infty} + \|L\|_{\infty} \cdot \|\delta U\|_{\infty} + \|\delta L\|_{\infty} \cdot \|\delta U\|_{\infty}$

and we have already bounded all the quantities on the right. These bounds combine with (21.38) to give

(21.41) **Theorem.** *The solution x computed by Gaussian elimination with pivoting satisfies the equation*

(21.1) $$(A + \delta A)x = b$$

where δA is defined by (21.40). Furthermore

(21.42) $$\|\delta A\|_{\infty} \leq 1.01(n^3 + 3n^2)\rho\,\|A\|_{\infty}\,u.$$

This is what we set out to show: that the x computed by Gaussian elimination with pivoting exactly satisfies a set of equations involving a perturbed matrix $A + \delta A$, and furthermore that the norm of the perturbation is no larger than some computable number involving the unit round-off times the norm of the original matrix.

Note that the perturbation δA depends upon b (because δU and δL depend upon b) but that the bound on $\|\delta A\|_\infty$ does not involve b. Also observe that for even approximate equality to hold in (21.42) the "worst" round-off must occur at each step of the calculation and, furthermore, equations like $\|L \, \delta U\|_\infty = \|L\|_\infty \cdot \|\delta U\|_\infty$ must hold. We know of no examples where $\|\delta A\|_\infty$ is even close to the given bound. Wilkinson (1963) states (p. 108) that $\|\delta A\|_\infty$ is rarely larger than $nu\|A\|_\infty$.

Theorem (21.41) can be used to obtain bounds for other measures of the error such as the residual, $b - Ax$, and $x - A^{-1}b$. We leave these as exercises.

(21.43) **Exercise.**   Derive (21.42) from (21.39) and (21.40).

(21.44) **Exercise.**   Use (21.41) to obtain an upper bound for the relative size of the residual,

$$\|b - Ax\|_\infty/\|x\|_\infty.$$

The bound should involve n, ρ, u and $\|A\|_\infty$.

(21.45) **Exercise.**   Use (21.41) to bound the relative error,

$$\|x - x^*\|_\infty/\|x\|_\infty.$$

Here $x^* = A^{-1}b$ is the exact solution to the problem. The bound should involve n, ρ, u, and the ∞-condition number of A, defined by $\text{cond}_\infty (A) = \|A\|_\infty \cdot \|A^{-1}\|_\infty$.

(21.46) **Exercise.**   Referring to (21.45), what can you say about

$$\|x - x^*\|_\infty/\|x^*\|_\infty\,?$$

(This is more difficult.)

(21.47) **Exercise.**   The residual $r = b - Ax$ can actually be computed (using accumulated inner products). Bound

$$\|x - x^*\|_\infty/\|x^*\|_\infty$$

in terms of $\|r\|_\infty$, $\|b\|_\infty$, and $\text{cond}_\infty (A)$. Equation (21.1) is not involved. This is an a posteriori error bound because it involves knowing the actual computed solution.

The basic rounding-error bound (21.27) for the triangular decomposition of A was derived in terms of partial pivoting. However, since the inequality (21.23) holds for either partial or complete pivoting, theorems (21.27) and (21.41) hold for either kind. The quantity ρ certainly depends on the actual algorithm used, including the type of pivoting.

Suppose that all $|a_{i,j}| \leq 1$. There are difficult and interesting open questions about how large the numbers $|a_{i,j}^{(k)}|$ can become during an elimination with complete pivoting. Let

$$(21.48) \qquad g(n) = \max_{i,j,k} |a_{i,j}^{(k)}|, \quad \text{where all} \quad |a_{i,j}| \leq 1.$$

Wilkinson (1961) proves that

$$(21.49) \qquad g(n) \leq 1.8 n^{(1/4)\ln n}, \quad \text{for all } n.$$

The bound of (21.49) is, of course, very much smaller than the best bound 2^{n-1} that can be given for partial pivoting. As we stated earlier, the bound 2^{n-1} can actually be attained with partial pivoting. On the other hand, the largest known value of $g(n)$ is only n, which can be achieved for certain matrices of arbitrarily high order. It is reasonable to conjecture that $g(n) \leq n$ for all real matrices, and this is certainly much smaller than the bound of (21.49). Tornheim (1965) has given examples of complex matrices A for which $g(n) \doteq 1.05n$, for arbitrarily high orders n.

22. CONVERGENCE OF ITERATIVE IMPROVEMENT

If, for some reason, we are not satisfied with the accuracy of the solution computed by Gaussian elimination, the technique of iterative improvement introduced in Sec. 13 can give us a very accurate answer in most cases, with a small amount of additional work. In this section we study iterative improvement in more detail and derive sufficient conditions for its convergence.

Let A and b be the given matrix and right-hand side. Let x_1 be the approximate solution vector obtained by Gaussian elimination. Then for $m = 1, 2, \ldots$ an improved solution x_{m+1} is obtained in the following way. First, the residual vector is calculated:

$$(22.1) \qquad r_m = b - Ax_m.$$

Then the correction vector is calculated by solving the system

$$(22.2) \qquad Ad_m = r_m,$$

using the LU decomposition for A found during the calculation of x_1. Finally, the correction is added to x_m to get an improved solution:

$$(22.3) \qquad x_{m+1} = x_m + d_m.$$

These three steps are repeated until, hopefully, x_m reaches the desired accuracy.

A complete analysis of this process is somewhat involved, and the important aspects tend to be lost in detail. Instead we have chosen to investigate an idealized version: *We assume that the only rounding errors occur in the calculation of the corrections from the residuals.* In other words, we assume that equations (22.1) and (22.3) hold exactly and that only (22.2) is affected by round-off error. This is a reasonable assumption if accumulated inner products are used for (22.1). A complete analysis for floating-point arithmetic without this simplifying assumption is given in Moler (1967).

Solving the system (22.2) is exactly the process we studied in the preceding chapter. There we found that round-off error replaces (22.2) with

$$(22.4) \qquad (A + \delta A)d_m = r_m,$$

where δA depends upon r_m but has a bound independent of r_m. In order to display this dependence upon m and simplify later expressions, we rewrite (22.4) as

$$(22.5) \qquad A(I + F_m)d_m = r_m,$$

where

$$(22.6) \qquad F_m = A^{-1}(\delta A).$$

As we might expect, the matrices F_m completely determine the behavior of this idealized version of iterative improvement.

(22.7) **Theorem.** *Let the vectors x_m be defined as above. Let x^* be the true solution of the linear system; that is, $x^* = A^{-1}b$. Assume that in some norm of Sec. 2*

$$\|F_m\| \le \sigma < \tfrac{1}{2}, \quad \text{for all } m.$$

Then the approximate solutions converge to the true solution; that is,

$$\|x_m - x^*\| \to 0, \quad as \quad m \to \infty.$$

We begin the proof by combining (22.1) and (22.5) to obtain

$$A(I + F_m)d_m = b - Ax_m.$$

Since A is nonsingular,

$$(I + F_m)d_m = x^* - x_m.$$

Hence, by (22.3),

$$(I + F_m)x_{m+1} = F_m x_m + x^*.$$

Subtracting $(I + F_m)x^*$ from both sides, we obtain

$$(22.8) \qquad (I + F_m)(x_{m+1} - x^*) = F_m(x_m - x^*).$$

Before we can proceed further we need the following lemma:

(22.9) **Lemma.** *Assume F is a matrix with $\|F\| < 1$, in some norm of Sec 2. Then*

(a) $\qquad\qquad\qquad I + F$ *is nonsingular,*

and

(b) $\qquad\qquad\qquad \|(I + F)^{-1}\| \le 1/(1 - \|F\|).$

To prove (a), assume $I + F$ is singular. Then there is some nonzero vector x with

$$(I + F)x = \theta.$$

This leads to

$$\|Fx\| = \|x\|,$$

which contradicts the assumption that $\|F\| < 1$.

To prove (b), let $G = (I + F)^{-1}$. Then $G = I - FG$, so that

$$\|G\| \leq \|I\| + \|F\| \cdot \|G\|$$

and, since $\|I\| = 1$, $\|G\| \leq 1/(1 - \|F\|).$

This completes the proof of lemma (22.9).

Returning to the proof of theorem (22.7), we note that our assumption that $\|F_m\| < \frac{1}{2}$ is more than sufficient to allow the application of the lemma to the matrices F_m. Thus, from (22.8),

(22.10) $$x_{m+1} - x^* = (I + F_m)^{-1}F_m(x_m - x^*).$$

This is the key equation of the section. It shows that the error at the $(m + 1)$-th step of the iteration is a certain (unknown) matrix times the error at the m-th step. If we had not assumed that (22.1) and (22.3) were exactly satisfied, there would be two additional terms in (22.10). (If we had assumed that (22.1), (22.2), and (22.3) were all exact, then F_m would be Θ and x_{m+1} would equal x^*.)

Applying part (b) of lemma (22.9) to (22.10), we obtain

(22.11)
$$\|x_{m+1} - x^*\| \leq \|F_m\|(1 - \|F_m\|)^{-1} \|x_m - x^*\|$$
$$\leq \sigma(1 - \sigma)^{-1} \|x_m - x^*\|.$$

If we let $\tau = \sigma/(1 - \sigma)$, then by induction

$$\|x_m - x^*\| \leq \tau^{m-1} \|x_1 - x^*\|.$$

We can go slightly further. If we let $x_0 = \theta$, we can say that x_1 is given by (22.3) with $m = 0$. Thus

$$\|x_1 - x^*\| \leq \tau \|x^*\|,$$

and hence

(22.12) $$\|x_m - x^*\| \leq \tau^m \|x^*\|.$$

The theorem then follows from (22.12) because $\sigma < \frac{1}{2}$ implies $\tau < 1$.

Since the matrices F_m are almost impossible to determine, it is usually impractical to check whether or not the hypothesis of theorem (22.7) is satisfied in any given situation. A slightly more practical result is the following:

(22.13) **Corollary.** *Assume*

$$1.01(n^3 + 3n^2)\rho u \|A\|_\infty \|A^{-1}\|_\infty < \tfrac{1}{2}.$$

Then $\|x_m - x^*\|_\infty \to 0$ *as* $m \to \infty$.

(See (21.24), (20.9), and (21.3) for the definitions of ρ, u, and $\|\cdot\|_\infty$.) It is possible to construct examples in which the hypothesis of the theorem (22.7) is satisfied while that of the corollary (22.13) is not.

The proof of (22.13) follows immediately from equations (21.42) and (22.6). The quantity $\text{cond}_\infty (A) = \|A\|_\infty \cdot \|A^{-1}\|_\infty$ is the condition of A with respect to the maximum norm. Thus corollary (22.13) is a precise version of the statement: "Iterative improvement converges if the matrix is not too badly conditioned."

Inequality (22.12) gives more than a proof of convergence—it also gives an estimate of the rate of convergence. The error at each step of the iteration is at most τ times the error at the previous step. For example, assume we have a computer like the IBM 7090 with 27-bit, chopping binary arithmetic. Then

$$u = 2^{-26} \doteq 10^{-8}.$$

Assume we have a 20-by-20 matrix with a condition number about 5×10^5. This is a fairly badly conditioned problem for this computer. Assume further that

$$\|\delta A\|_\infty \doteq nu \|A\|_\infty,$$

so that

$$\|F_m\|_\infty \doteq nu \, \text{cond}_\infty (A) \doteq .1,$$

and hence

$$\tau \doteq \|F_m\|_\infty /(1 - \|F_m\|_\infty) \doteq .1.$$

Then the inequality

$$\|x_1 - x^*\|_\infty \leq \tau \|x^*\|_\infty$$

indicates that the first approximation is correct to about one decimal place, while the relation

$$\|x_8 - x^*\|_\infty \leq \tau^8 \|x^*\|_\infty$$

indicates that the eighth approximation is correct to about as many figures as our computer will hold.

If we carry this example any further, we find one major defect of our idealized analysis. Theorem (22.7) claims that by taking enough iterations it is possible to make the error $\|x_m - x^*\|_\infty$ arbitrarily small. This is clearly not possible because the components of the vector x_m must be single-precision floating-point numbers, whereas, in general, the components of x^* are not. A little thought will reveal that the difficulty comes from our assumption that (22.3) is exactly satisfied. In practice, we make a rounding error in each component at this step, so we can never correct x_m beyond the unit round-off level. A more detailed analysis would lead to something like

$$(22.14) \qquad \|x_m - x^*\|_\infty \leq \left(\tau^m + \frac{u}{1-\tau} \right) \|x^*\|_\infty$$

in place of (22.12). We would not find that the error approaches zero but only that it gets small.

Finally, we again emphasize the need for precise calculation of the residuals. We have assumed that (22.1) is exact. This is a reasonable approximation if we use extended-precision inner products to calculate the residuals. However, if ordinary floating-point arithmetic is used, almost all accuracy will be lost in the subtraction $b_i - \sum_{j=1}^{n} a_{i,j} x_j$, and the calculated residuals will bear little relation to their true value.

(22.15) **Exercise.** Revise (22.3) to include a term which accounts for the round-off error. Revise the proof of theorem (22.7) to take this additional term into consideration.

(22.16) **Exercise.** Suppose A is a square matrix. Suppose an approximate inverse X has the properties

$$\|AX - I\| \leq .01,$$

$$\|X\| = 200.$$

Give a rigorous upper bound for $\|X - A^{-1}\|$ that is reasonably sharp. (One answer: 2.03.)

23. POSITIVE DEFINITE MATRICES; BAND MATRICES

Several special types of matrices occur in so many problems that it is desirable to take advantage of their particular properties. In this section we will consider two of these—positive definite matrices and band matrices.

In Sec. 9 we concluded that any positive definite matrix A has a unique decomposition in the form

$$(23.1) \qquad A = GG^T,$$

where G is a lower triangular matrix with positive diagonal elements. In particular, positive definiteness implies the nonsingularity of the minors necessary for the LU theorem. Writing each element of (23.1), we see that if $a_{j,j}$ is on the main diagonal of A then

$$(23.2) \qquad a_{j,j} = g_{j,1}^2 + g_{j,2}^2 + \cdots + g_{j,j}^2$$

and, if $a_{i,j}$ is below the diagonal, then

$$(23.3) \qquad a_{i,j} = g_{i,1}g_{j,1} + g_{i,2}g_{j,2} + \cdots + g_{i,j}g_{j,j} \quad (j < i).$$

Used in a correct order, these equations can determine all the elements of G. One proper order is: $g_{1,1}, g_{2,1}, \ldots, g_{n,1}, g_{2,2}, g_{3,2}, \ldots, g_{n,2}, g_{3,3}, \ldots, g_{n,n}$. Equation (23.2) is used for a diagonal element of G, and then (23.3) is used for the off-diagonal elements in the same column. This yields the algorithm:

$$(23.4)$$

for $j := 1$ **step** 1 **until** n **do**
begin $g_{j,j} := sqrt\,(a_{j,j} - \sum_{k=1}^{j-1} g_{j,k}^2);$
$\quad$ **for** $i := j + 1$ **step** 1 **until** n **do**
$\quad\quad g_{i,j} := (a_{i,j} - \sum_{k=1}^{j-1} g_{i,k}g_{j,k})/g_{j,j};$
end.

Notice that the elements of A above the diagonal are not involved because of the symmetry.

This algorithm is *Cholesky's method* or the *square-root method* for factoring a positive definite matrix; see Faddeev and Faddeeva (1963). Part of its usefulness lies in the fact that it is not necessary to search for pivots. For matrices which are not positive definite a search for pivots is necessary because we divide by these pivots and must be sure that elements of the

114

reduced matrix are not too large. Any large elements would lead to large rounding errors and loss of accuracy. However, in Cholesky's method for positive definite matrices we need only refer to equation (23.2) to see that

$$(23.5) \qquad\qquad |g_{i,j}| \le \sqrt{a_{i,i}}$$

for any i, j. In other words, the elements of G are bounded, even when pivoting is not used.

Use of a similar method for matrices which are not positive definite is not possible without complex arithmetic because (23.1) does not hold in general. Even if A were symmetric, the algorithm would break down because it would call for division by zero or for the square root of a negative number. (If A were positive definite but very badly conditioned, rounding errors might destroy the definiteness. This would also lead to square roots of negative numbers and the necessary termination of the algorithm.)

Because of the symmetry of A it is necessary to store only $\frac{1}{2}n(n + 1)$, or slightly over half, of its elements, resulting in an important saving of computer storage for large matrices. But in order to take advantage of this saving, a relatively complicated subscripting scheme is usually necessary, with consequent loss of time.

In Sec. 6 we described a *band matrix* of band width $2m + 1$ as one for which $a_{i,j} = 0$ if $|i - j| > m$. For example, if $m = 1$ the band width is three and the matrix has the following form:

$$(23.6) \qquad
\begin{bmatrix}
a_{1,1} & a_{1,2} & & & & & \\
a_{2,1} & a_{2,2} & a_{2,3} & & & & \\
& a_{3,2} & a_{3,3} & a_{3,4} & & & \\
& & \cdot & \cdot & \cdot & & \\
& & & \cdot & \cdot & \cdot & \\
& & & & \cdot & \cdot & \cdot \\
& & & & & \cdot & a_{n,n-1} \\
& & & & & a_{n-1,n} & a_{n,n}
\end{bmatrix}$$

Such a matrix is also called *tridiagonal*.

The concept of a band matrix is useful only if m is appreciably smaller than n. After all, any matrix is a band matrix with $m = n - 1$. (Matrices with comparatively few zero elements are called dense matrices in order to contrast them with band matrices or sparse matrices; see Sec. 6.) The width of the band depends upon the ordering of the unknowns and the equations in the system. For example, interchanging the second and third rows (equations) in (23.6) increases the band width from three to five.

By taking advantage of the band structure, a linear equation solver can save both time and space. Space is saved because only the nonzero part of the matrix needs to be stored in the computer. Such a storage arrangement requires $(2m + 1)n$ locations, compared with n^2 for a full matrix. Thus storage space is saved if m is less than $(n - 1)/2$. One way to accomplish this within the typical rectangular data structures of computers is to let

$$(23.7) \qquad c_{i,j} = a_{i,i+j}, \quad i = 1, \ldots, n; \quad j = -m, \ldots, 0, \ldots, m.$$

The array C then occupies $(2m + 1)n$ locations. (The elements $c_{i,j}$ with $i + j < 0$ or $i + j > n$ are not defined but still occupy storage locations.) For very small m it may be convenient instead to use $2m + 1$ vectors. The band of (23.6) could be stored in three vectors—for example, d, e, and f—as follows:

$$(23.8) \qquad \begin{bmatrix} e_1 & f_1 & & & & & \\ d_2 & e_2 & f_2 & & & & \\ & d_3 & e_3 & f_3 & & & \\ & & \cdot & \cdot & \cdot & & \\ & & & \cdot & \cdot & \cdot & \\ & & & & \cdot & \cdot & f_{n-1} \\ & & & & & d_n & e_n \end{bmatrix}$$

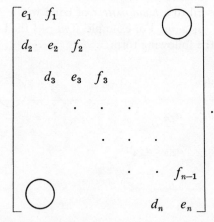

The compact storage arrangements would not be very useful if they could not be retained during the solution of a system of equations. Fortunately, they can be.

(23.9) **Theorem.** *If a band matrix with band width $2m + 1$ has an LU decomposition, then $L = (l_{i,j})$ and $U = (u_{i,j})$ are triangular band matrices. That is,*

$$l_{i,j} \neq 0 \quad only\ for \quad i = j - m, \ldots, j,$$
$$u_{i,j} \neq 0 \quad only\ for \quad i = j, \ldots, j + m.$$

The proof follows that of theorem (9.2), so we omit it. When $m = 1$, the matrices L and U have the forms

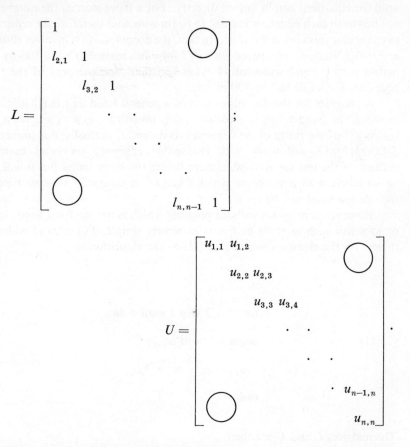

$$L = \begin{bmatrix} 1 & & & & & \\ l_{2,1} & 1 & & & & \\ & l_{3,2} & 1 & & & \\ & & \cdot & \cdot & & \\ & & & \cdot & \cdot & \\ & & & & \cdot & \\ & & & & l_{n,n-1} & 1 \end{bmatrix};$$

$$U = \begin{bmatrix} u_{1,1} & u_{1,2} & & & & \\ & u_{2,2} & u_{2,3} & & & \\ & & u_{3,3} & u_{3,4} & & \\ & & & \cdot & \cdot & \\ & & & & \cdot & \cdot \\ & & & & & u_{n-1,n} \\ & & & & & u_{n,n} \end{bmatrix}$$

We assumed in theorem (23.9) that the LU decomposition of the matrix exists. Of course, this is not always so, and it may be necessary to interchange equations—to pivot—in order to assure the existence and accuracy of L and U. This interchange will usually increase the band width, but it cannot do more than double it. The matrices L and U will still have a band structure but with a larger value of m.

For some band matrices that occur in practice pivoting is not necessary. The matrices obtained by finite-difference approximations to differential equations, for example, are often irreducible (6.4) and diagonally dominant (6.1). It can be shown that pivoting is not necessary for such matrices.

(23.10) **Exercise.** Prove that pivoting is unnecessary for irreducible, diagonally dominant matrices. See Wendroff (1966).

Using the band structure of L and U saves time also. The purpose of Gaussian elimination is to reduce the number of unknowns in each equation until the equations can be solved directly. For a band matrix, the number of unknowns in each equation is small to begin with, and therefore the reduction to triangular form takes less time. In fact, the decomposition involves roughly nm^2 multiplications, compared with $n^3/3$ for a full matrix. Thus a 100-by-100 matrix with a band width of 11 takes less than one per cent of the time necessary for a full 100-by-100 matrix.

A program for the decomposition of a general band matrix (that is, one in which the band width is a parameter) is much the same as one for a full matrix. Only the range of the subscripts is different. Actually, our procedure *DECOMPOSE* will work with reasonable efficiency on band matrices because of the test for zero multipliers before the inner loop. But it will not be so efficient as a program which "knows in advance" that multipliers outside the band will be zero.

However, a program without pivoting which is written for a fixed, small band width such as three or five is extremely simple. For a band width of three with the elements stored as in (23.8) the algorithm is

$$u_1 := e_1;$$

for $i := 2$ **step** 1 **until** n **do**

(23.11)   **begin** $m_i := d_i/u_{i-1};$

$$u_i := e_i - m_i \times f_{i-1};$$

end.

The matrices L and U are then

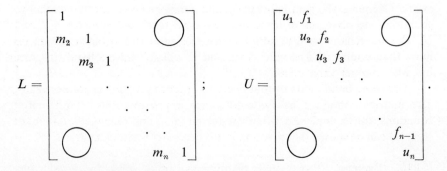

The subsequent solution of the system $Ax = LUx = b$ is also very simple.

We have

$$x_1 := b_1;$$

for $i := 2$ **step** 1 **until** n **do**

$$x_i := b_i - m_i \times x_{i-1};$$

(23.12)

$$x_n := x_n/u_n;$$

for $i := n - 1$ **step** $- 1$ **until** 1 **do**

$$x_i := (x_i - f_i \times x_{i+1})/u_i.$$

The algorithm (23.11) must be used with care, however, because it does not pivot. (Some of the u_i may be zero.)

Because only a few arithmetic operations are involved in solving a system of equations with a band matrix, it is usually not necessary to use iterative improvement. In this case storage space can be saved by overwriting A with L and U. In (23.11) the arrays m and u can simply replace d and e.

If pivoting is used, then U itself will involve as much storage as A if the band width doubles. In this case either additional storage must be provided for L or the right-hand sides must be processed simultaneously and L not saved.

(23.13) **Exercise.** Write programs *CHOLESKY DECOMPOSE* (n, A, G) and *CHOLESKY SOLVE* (n, G, b, x) to use in place of *DECOMPOSE* and *SOLVE* for positive definite matrices. Note that *IMPROVE* requires no changes.

(23.14) **Exercise.** Prove that symmetric, irreducible, diagonally dominant matrices with positive diagonal elements are positive definite.

(23.15) **Exercise.** Show that pivoting is not necessary when using Gaussian elimination with positive definite matrices.

(23.16) **Exercise.** Write a program *BAND* (n, m, C, b, x) which accepts a general band matrix, stored as in (23.7), and solves the system $Ax = b$. Use pivoting and do not save the elements of L. Do not use any more array storage than that provided by the parameters.

24. ITERATIVE METHODS FOR SOLVING LINEAR SYSTEMS

When practical linear equation systems are of a very large order, they are generally sparse. For example, the solution of the Dirichlet problem for Laplace's partial differential equation might be approximated by finite-difference equations over a network with 5000 points. The corresponding matrix is of order 5000, so there are 25,000,000 elements in the matrix. However, only about 25,000 of these differ from zero. Even these 25,000 nonzero elements do not have to be stored because their values are known directly from the geometry of the difference network. With such a matrix, Gaussian elimination has an overwhelming disadvantage because it changes many of the zero elements to nonzero values. Moreover, it changes the simple nonzero elements to complicated values which must be stored. Thus in the above example the user of Gaussian elimination has to contend with storing more than 100,000 matrix elements.

In contrast to Gaussian elimination there are a number of methods for solving linear systems $Ax = b$ which make use only of the original matrix A. These methods consist of relatively simple algorithms for converting any vector $x^{(k)}$ into another vector $x^{(k+1)}$ which depends on $x^{(k)}$, on A, and on b. (With some iterations $x^{(k+1)}$ may depend on other vectors $x^{(k-r)}$ for $r > 0$, but we shall not consider this possibility here.) A substantial treatment of iterative methods forms the main part of several books, and we can hardly do more than hint at them here.

To give the reader an idea of the equations for which iterative techniques are used, we shall describe a problem in partial differential equations and then replace this problem by a simple finite-difference scheme. It is not important for the reader to have a background in partial differential equations. Much more is written about this subject in Forsythe and Wasow (1960).

Let R be the 4-by-3 open rectangle

$$R = \{(x, y) \mid 0 < x < 4 \quad \text{and} \quad 0 < y < 3\}.$$

Let $\bar{R}$ be the closed rectangle which is the closure of R:

$$\bar{R} = \{(x, y) \mid 0 \leq x \leq 4 \quad \text{and} \quad 0 \leq y \leq 3\}.$$

Let B denote the boundary of R, omitting the four corners. We write B as the union of two sets T and S. Here T is the "top" of the rectangle, and S is the other sides. See fig. (24.3). We have

$$T = \{(x, y) \mid 0 < x < 4 \quad \text{and} \quad y = 3\};$$
$$S = \{(x, y) \mid (0 < x < 4 \quad \text{and} \quad y = 0)$$
$$\text{or} \quad (x = 0 \quad \text{and} \quad 0 < y < 3)$$
$$\text{or} \quad (x = 4 \quad \text{and} \quad 0 < y < 3)\};$$
$$B = T \cup S.$$

The problem is to find a function $u = u(x, y)$ defined on $\bar{R}$ so that

(24.1)
$$\frac{\partial^2 u}{\partial x^2} + \frac{\partial^2 u}{\partial y^2} = 0 \quad \text{in } R$$

with boundary conditions

(24.2)
$$\begin{cases} u = 1 \quad \text{on } T \\ u = 0 \quad \text{on } S. \end{cases}$$

(24.3)

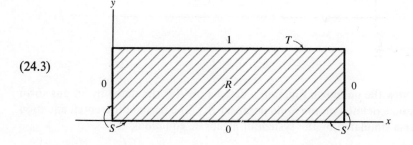

The problem (24.1, 24.2) is called a *Dirichlet problem* for Laplace's differential equation. Heat distribution is one frequent source of such problems. Suppose a very long homogeneous metal bar has $\bar{R}$ as its cross section and that the bar is held at the temperature $1°$ everywhere on the face corresponding to T and at $0°$ everywhere on the three faces corresponding to S. Then the steady-state temperature inside the bar will satisfy the equation system (24.1, 24.2).

There are many ways to solve problems like (24.1, 24.2) approximately. One method of great general applicability is the so-called *method of finite differences*. We may look upon this as consisting of a finite simulation of the original problem. It might proceed as follows: Let N be a positive integer, and let $h = 1/N$. We first simulate R by the rectangular array R_h of

$(3N - 1)(4N - 1)$ points:

$$R_h = \left\{ \left(\frac{i}{N}, \frac{j}{N} \right) \ \middle| \ i = 1, 2, \ldots, 4N - 1 \quad \text{and} \quad j = 1, 2, \ldots, 3N - 1 \right\}.$$

Similarly, we simulate T by the linear array of $4N - 1$ points:

$$T_h = \{ (i/N, 3) \ | \ i = 1, 2, \ldots, 4N - 1 \}.$$

Also, let S_h denote the set of all points $(i/N, j/N)$ which lie in S. Let $\bar{R}_h = R_h \cup T_h \cup S_h$. See fig. (24.4) for $N = 1$.

(24.4)

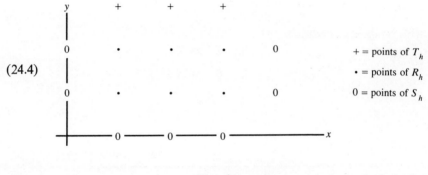

$$N = 1$$

Now the unknown function u defined on $\bar{R}$ is simulated by an unknown function v defined on the finite point set $\bar{R}_h$. The partial differential equation (24.1) is simulated by the system of algebraic equations

$$\frac{v(x - h, y) - 2v(x, y) + v(x + h, y)}{h^2}$$
$$+ \frac{v(x, y - h) - 2v(x, y) + v(x, y + h)}{h^2} = 0$$

for each (x, y) in R_h. These divided differences give excellent approximations to $\partial^2 v/\partial x^2$, $\partial^2 v/\partial y^2$, respectively, for any smooth function $v(x, y)$ defined on all of R. The boundary conditions (24.2) are simulated by setting $v = 1$ on T_h and $v = 0$ on S_h.

Thus our partial differential equation problem (24.1, 24.2) is replaced by an algebraic problem for each integer N—namely, to find v defined on $\bar{R}_h$ so that

(24.5) $4v(x, y) - v(x, y + h) - v(x - h, y) -$
$\qquad v(x, y - h) - v(x + h, y) = 0$ for each (x, y) in R_h,

with

(24.6) $v(x, y) = 1$ on T_h and $v(x, y) = 0$ on S_h.

With a contemporary computer one could easily store over 15,000 net points. Thus, setting $(3N + 1)(4N + 1)$ approximately equal to 15,000, we might actually solve the system (24.5, 24.6) with $N = 34$. We note that there are $n = (3N - 1)(4N - 1)$ unknown function values in the system. Thus the matrix corresponding to the system (24.5, 24.6) is of order n, and therefore it has $n^2 = (3N - 1)^2(4N - 1)^2 \doteq 144N^4$ elements. However, only five or fewer elements differ from zero in each row of the matrix. Thus the density of the matrix is approximately $5/(12N^2)$.

To illustrate some aspects of solving such a system, we shall set $N = 1$ so that there are six points in R_h as in fig. (24.7), where the ten points of T_h and S_h are also shown by the corresponding boundary values.

(24.7)

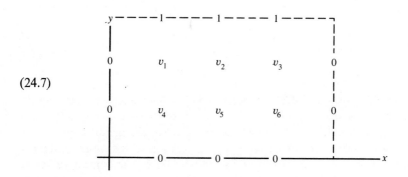

With the six unknown values of v numbered as in fig. (24.7), the equation system (24.5, 24.6) can be written

(24.8)

$$
\left\{
\begin{array}{l}
4v_1 - v_2 \quad\quad - v_4 \quad\quad\quad\quad\quad = 1 \\
- v_1 + 4v_2 - v_3 \quad\quad - v_5 \quad\quad = 1 \\
\quad\quad - v_2 + 4v_3 \quad\quad\quad\quad - v_6 = 1 \\
- v_1 \quad\quad\quad\quad + 4v_4 - v_5 \quad\quad = 0 \\
\quad\quad - v_2 \quad\quad\quad - v_4 + 4v_5 - v_6 = 0 \\
\quad\quad\quad\quad - v_3 \quad\quad\quad - v_5 + 4v_6 = 0.
\end{array}
\right.
$$

Note that 16 of the 36 coefficients in (24.8) are equal to zero. Although system (24.8) could readily be solved in any number of ways, including Gaussian elimination, we shall illustrate the application of some iterative methods to its solution—methods which might be used on a computer for much larger values of N.

(24.9) **Exercise.** Prove that (24.8) has a unique solution. *Hint:* Assume there were two distinct solution vectors w and y, and let $z = w - y$. Then z would satisfy an equation system like (24.8) with a right-hand side of all zeros. Show that this implies that $z = 0$. See exercise (23.14).

In any iterative method for solving the system (24.5, 24.6), one starts with some reasonable or convenient set of values for the v_i. Let us take the values $v_1 = v_3 = .400$, $v_2 = .600$, $v_4 = v_6 = .100$, $v_5 = .300$. To illustrate:

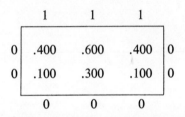

We shall now describe a process which goes under various names: the *Gauss-Seidel method, Liebmann's method,* or the *method of successive displacements.* We first fix the order in which we will change the components v_i. Here we shall use the order $v_1, v_2, v_3, v_4, v_5, v_6$ in which we have already numbered them. Now we change v_1 as follows: Using the current values of v_2, v_3, v_4, v_5, v_6 and the boundary values, the value of $v_1 = v(1, 2)$ is recomputed so that equation (24.5) is satisfied with $(x, y) = (1, 2)$. That is, at this stage, we define a new v_1 so that

(24.10) $$4v_1 - 0 - v_4 - v_2 - 1 = 0,$$

where v_2 and v_4 are taken at the initial values—namely, $v_2 = .600$, $v_4 = .100$. Solving (24.10) for v_1, we have

(24.11) $$v_1 := (1 + 0 + v_4 + v_2)/4.$$

Just to be precise about the arithmetic, we shall evaluate (24.11) and analogous formulas below in three-decimal, floating-point arithmetic, computing from left to right. Then we get from (24.11) that $v_1 = .425$, which immediately replaces the old value of v_1.

We now proceed to evaluate v_2 so that it satisfies the equation (24.5) with $(x, y) = (2, 2)$. We have

$$v_2 := (1 + v_1 + v_5 + v_3)/4;$$

i.e.,

$$v_2 := (1.00 + .425 + .300 + .400)/4$$

$$= (1.43 + .300 + .400)/4$$

$$= (2.13)/4$$

$$= .533.$$

The arithmetic is carefully rounded to three significant decimal digits.
Next, we have

$$v_3 := (1 + v_2 + v_6 + 0)/4$$

$$= (1.00 + .533 + .100)/4$$

$$= .408;$$

$$v_4 := (v_1 + 0 + 0 + v_5)/4$$

$$= (.425 + .300)/4$$

$$= .181;$$

$$v_5 := (v_2 + v_4 + 0 + v_6)/4$$

$$= (.533 + .181 + .100)/4$$

$$= .204;$$

$$v_6 := (v_3 + v_5 + 0 + 0)/4$$

$$= (.408 + .204)/4$$

$$= .153.$$

At this point we have completed one cycle of the iteration, having replaced all the v_i with new values. The word "successive" in successive displacements refers to the fact that each v_i is replaced by its new value before the next v_i is computed. Here is the picture after the first cycle:

	1	1	1	
0	.425	.533	.408	0
0	.181	.204	.153	0
	0	0	0	

The iteration continues in the same way for more cycles. We give only the results of each cycle:

	1	1	1	
0	.428	.510	.415	0
0	.158	.205	.155	0
	0	0	0	

	1	1	1	
0	.418	.513	.418	0
0	.156	.206	.156	0
	0	0	0	

	1	1	1	
0	.418	.513	.418	0
0	.156	.206	.156	0
	0	0	0	

Note that the v_i do not change in the fourth cycle. Hence there will be no further change, and the computational results have converged to a limiting state. When this occurs, we have accomplished all that we can with ordinary three-decimal, floating-point arithmetic.

It is not difficult to show that our averaging process causes every component v_i to remain between the greatest and least of the initial values of the v_i and the boundary values, except for possible small effects of round-off. It is then possible to show that there are only a finite number of different vectors v attainable in a given iteration. Hence the sequence of values of the vector v after the successive cycles of the iteration must eventually either reach a fixed terminal state (as in our example above) or enter a periodic phase in which the vectors repeat themselves after a fixed number of cycles. We believe that either of these two terminations of the iteration is possible but have no information as to which occurs more often.

(24.12) **Exercise.** Solve the same problem in three-decimal floating-point arithmetic with the initial vector $v_1 = v_2 = v_3 = v_4 = v_5 = v_6 = 0$. Show that one gets the same answer in seven cycles.

The fact that our floating-point iteration converges to a fixed limiting vector should not lead us to believe that the limit is the correctly rounded answer to the problem (24.8). The rounding error can be bounded by the techniques of Secs. 22 and 23, but we shall not go into this.

The unwary numerical analyst is likely to assume that the error will be at most one digit in the last place. However, the correctly rounded five-decimal solution to our small problem is

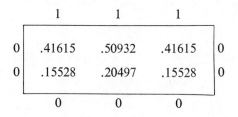

Note that the largest error of our three-decimal limit vector is .00368, which is almost four units in the last decimal place. As with Gaussian elimination, the error in our three-decimal arithmetic could be greatly reduced by carrying out the basic operation of (24.11) and analogous later formulas with double-precision accumulation in the numerator, followed by a rounded division of four into the double-precision number. If this had been done, starting from the final stage of the previous iteration, we would have converged to

	1	1	1	
0	.417	.510	.417	0
0	.156	.206	.156	0
	0	0	0	

in one more iteration. Note that the maximum error is now .00103, which is less than one-third as large as the maximum error without the double-precision accumulation.

A complete study of any iteration in the presence of round-off is extremely difficult and has rarely been done. It is much easier to study the same iteration in exact arithmetic, without any rounding off. This provides a very useful mathematical model of the behavior of the actual rounded iteration, a model which within limits is an excellent indicator of the actual behavior of a rounded iteration until the error has been reduced to the general level of the round-off "noise."

In the absence of round-off the iterative process we have described will produce an infinite sequence of (usually) ever-changing vectors, which we call

$v^{(0)}, v^{(1)}, v^{(2)}, \ldots, v^{(k)}, v^{(k+1)}, \ldots$. We wish to investigate the conditions under which $\{v^{(k)}\}$ is a convergent sequence of vectors.

It is instructive to express the iteration in terms of the equation system (24.8). Let $v^{(k)} = (v_1^{(k)}, \ldots, v_6^{(k)})$ be the result of the k-th cycle of iteration. The reader can easily show that the vector $v^{(k+1)}$ satisfies the equation system

$$(24.13) \quad \begin{cases} 4v_1^{(k+1)} - v_2^{(k)} & - v_4^{(k)} & = 1 \\ -v_1^{(k+1)} + 4v_2^{(k+1)} - v_3^{(k)} & -v_5^{(k)} & = 1 \\ - v_2^{(k+1)} + 4v_3^{(k+1)} & - v_6^{(k)} & = 1 \\ -v_1^{(k+1)} & + 4v_4^{(k+1)} - v_5^{(k)} & = 0 \\ - v_2^{(k+1)} & - v_4^{(k+1)} + 4v_5^{(k+1)} - v_6^{(k)} & = 0 \\ - v_3^{(k+1)} & - v_5^{(k+1)} + 4v_6^{(k+1)} & = 0. \end{cases}$$

The important thing to notice is that all components of v corresponding to matrix elements on and below the main diagonal have the superscript $k + 1$, whereas those corresponding to elements above the main diagonal have the superscript k. This reflects the fact that each component v_i is replaced by its new value in all subsequent computations.

We now express (24.13) in terms of matrices, in a form which can be generalized to any system of linear equations. Let the coefficient matrix of (24.13) be called A. Let the matrix A be expressed as the sum of two matrices F and G. Here F is a lower triangular matrix consisting of the elements of A on and below the main diagonal, with zeros inserted above the main diagonal. And G is an upper triangular matrix with zeros on and below the main diagonal and the elements of A above the main diagonal. Thus

$$(24.14) \qquad\qquad A = F + G.$$

Let the right-hand side of (24.13) be called the vector b. Then the system (24.8) can be written as the equation system $Av = b$. And the rule (24.13) for the iterative process can be written

$$(24.15) \qquad\qquad Fv^{(k+1)} + Gv^{(k)} = b.$$

To study the convergence of $v^{(k)}$, we let $e^{(k)}$ be the *error* in $v^{(k)}$ as a solution of (24.13):

$$e^{(k)} = v^{(k)} - v, \quad \text{where} \quad v = A^{-1}b.$$

Subtracting (24.15) from the identity $Fv + Gv = b$, we see that

$$(24.16) \qquad\qquad Fe^{(k+1)} + Ge^{(k)} = \theta.$$

If no diagonal element $a_{i,i}$ of A is zero, the matrix F is nonsingular and we may define a new matrix $H = -F^{-1}G$. Then from (24.16) we have

(24.17) $$e^{(k+1)} = He^{(k)}.$$

Finally, applying (24.17) we can prove by induction the final result

(24.18) $$e^{(k)} = H^k e^{(0)}.$$

We conclude that for a given $v^{(0)}$ the error $e^{(k)}$ goes to θ as $k \to \infty$ if and only if $H^k e^{(0)} \to \theta$ as $k \to \infty$, where $e^{(0)} = v^{(0)} - A^{-1}b$. Since $A^{-1}b$ is unknown, it is impractical to check whether $H^k e^{(0)} \to \theta$ for just one vector $e^{(0)}$. A more useful general result is as follows:

(24.19)   **Theorem.**   *Let A be a matrix with no $a_{i,i} = 0$. Suppose we use exact arithmetic in the iterative process of successive displacements. Then $v^{(k)} \to A^{-1}b$ as $k \to \infty$ for all initial vectors $v^{(0)}$ if and only if $H^k w \to \theta$ as $k \to \infty$ for all vectors w.*

We remind the reader of an important theorem of matrix theory:

(24.20)   **Theorem.**   *If H is an n-by-n matrix, then $H^k x \to \theta$ as $k \to \infty$ for every vector x if and only if each eigenvalue λ_i of H is less than one in modulus.*

For a proof of (24.20) the reader is referred, for example, to Forsythe and Wasow (1960). The essential idea is that by a similarity transformation H may be changed to a blockwise diagonal matrix $S^{-1}HS$ (the Jordan canonical form of H), each of whose diagonal blocks has the form

(24.21)

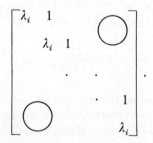

One then has only to prove the theorem for an arbitrary block of form (24.21).

   It follows from (24.19) and (24.20) that a necessary and sufficient condition for the convergence of the method of successive displacements is that all eigenvalues of $-F^{-1}G$ be less than one in modulus.

(24.22) **Exercise.** Prove that a necessary and sufficient condition for the convergence of the method of successive displacements is that all roots of

$$\det (\lambda F + G) = 0$$

be less than one in modulus.

Neither of these last two conditions is easy to check in most practical situations, and for general matrices it is by no means easy to decide whether the method of successive displacements will be convergent.

For the matrix A of (24.8) or its extension to general N, the method of successive displacements does in fact converge. There are several different ways of proving this. Some use a general theorem which assures convergence whenever A is a positive definite, symmetric matrix. See Forsythe and Wasow (1960). Others use a general theorem which assures convergence for any irreducible and diagonally dominant matrix A; see (6.1) and (6.4) for definitions of these terms and compare exercise (23.10). We shall not give any proof here. Also see Varga (1962).

There is another consequence of (24.18). Suppose, to simplify the illustration, that H has a unique real eigenvalue λ_1 of maximum modulus among the eigenvalues, with a corresponding eigenvector w, so that

$$Hw = \lambda_1 w.$$

It is then not difficult to prove that

(24.23) $$e^{(k)} = H^k e^{(0)} \doteq c\lambda_1^k w \quad \text{as} \quad k \to \infty,$$

for some constant c. To be more precise, $\|e^{(k)} - c\lambda_1^k w\|/\|e^{(k)}\| \to 0$ as $k \to \infty$. Ordinarily, for a problem of substantial size, $|\lambda_1|$ is close to one and the convergence of $e^{(k)}$ to θ is extremely slow. For example, as $N \to \infty$, it can be shown for our problem (24.5, 24.6) that

$$\lambda_1 \sim 1 - \frac{25\pi^2}{144N^2} \doteq 1 - \frac{1.7}{N^2} .$$

Because convergence of the method of successive displacements is so slow, the programmer must normally give attention to the "acceleration" of $v^{(k)}$ to θ, based on (24.23) and related equations. The design and use of acceleration techniques are important in applying iterative methods. We cannot go into the subject here.

If a computer memory is so organized that $v^{(k)}$ is stored in a "read-only" storage device, it may be more convenient to use the values of one fixed $v^{(k)}$ for all stages in the calculation of $v^{(k+1)}$. For example, it might be convenient to have all of $v^{(k)}$ on a magnetic tape, read it, generate all components of $v^{(k+1)}$, and store them on another tape—all in one pass, from equations of the form

$$(24.24) \quad \sum_{j=1}^{i-1} a_{i,j} v_j^{(k)} + a_{i,i} v_i^{(k+1)} + \sum_{j=i+1}^{n} a_{i,j} v_j^{(k)} = b_i, \quad (i = 1, 2, \ldots, n).$$

Note that equations (24.24) differ from (24.13) in that *all* off-diagonal components v_i in (24.24) are associated with the old vector $v^{(k)}$. This iteration, known as the *method of simultaneous displacements* or the *Jacobi method*, can also be written in the form (24.15), where we must now understand F to be the matrix of diagonal elements of A. In terms of this changed F, we can state the convergence tests (24.20) and (24.22). There are interesting theorems comparing the methods of simultaneous and successive displacements. See Varga (1962).

Sometimes equation systems like (24.8) are solved approximately by means of electrical networks or other analog devices. Normally these methods are closely related to the method of simultaneous displacements since electrical currents flow at the same time throughout the entire network.

A more sophisticated iterative method is called *successive overrelaxation* (SOR). This is a variant of the method of successive displacements in which each component v_i, in its turn, is changed not by the exact amount Δv_i necessary for the i-th equation to be solved exactly, but instead by the amount $\omega \cdot \Delta v_i$, where ω $(1 < \omega < 2)$ is chosen in such a way that the convergence of $v^{(k)}$ is accomplished asymptotically as fast as possible as $k \to \infty$. See Forsythe and Wasow (1960) for an exposition of this method, which for equation systems like (24.8) converges much faster than the method of successive displacements.

We emphasize the fact that for large and sparse matrices the matrix A is normally not stored as an array of n^2 elements in the computer store. At most the nonzero elements of A are stored, and for simple operators the elements need not be stored at all. Rather, they are generated as needed. Often an exception must be made for the elements of A corresponding to net points near the boundary of a region or at interfaces between different media. But the principal demand for storage is for the current vector $x^{(k)}$ and sometimes also for the right member b. This is why saving the storage of one vector x can so substantially reduce the storage problem for an iterative process.

25. NONLINEAR SYSTEMS OF EQUATIONS

One frequently has to solve a nonlinear system of simultaneous algebraic or transcendental equations. Let these be written

(25.1)
$$\begin{cases} f_1(x_1, \ldots, x_n) = 0 \\ \quad \cdot \quad \cdot \quad \cdot \quad \cdot \quad \cdot \\ f_n(x_1, \ldots, x_n) = 0. \end{cases}$$

Or, in vector form,

(25.2)
$$f(x) = 0.$$

There is no longer a simple theory that tells us whether solutions of (25.1) exist or whether they are unique. If the f_i are polynomials in the x_j, one can frequently give a bound for the total number of vector solutions x in complex, projective n space, and sometimes this helps assure us that we have located all of them.

However, ordinarily each nonlinear system must be treated as a special problem. One usually needs a reasonable first approximation to a solution, and then he can improve it.

There are two general methods for solving the system (25.1): the descent methods and the Newton methods.

In descent methods, one forms a real-valued function which is zero at any solution and positive otherwise. One such function is

(25.3)
$$G(x_1, \ldots, x_n) = \sum_{i=1}^{n} |f_i(x_1, \ldots, x_n)|^2.$$

Then solving (25.1) is reduced to finding minima of the function G, and, in particular, minima with value zero.

To minimize a function $G(x) = G(x_1, \ldots, x_n)$ by descent methods, one starts with some initial guess x^0, which is likely to be furnished by the problem originator. One then seeks a direction d^0 so that $G(x) - G(x^0) < 0$ for vectors x of form $x^0 + \alpha d^0$, for small enough values of $\alpha > 0$. One very good direction is

$$d^0 = -\text{grad } G(x) \quad \text{at } x^0,$$

where grad $G(x)$ is the vector

$$\left(\frac{\partial G}{\partial x_1}, \ldots, \frac{\partial G}{\partial x_n} \right)^T.$$

As shown in calculus, grad $G(x)$ is the direction in which $G(x)$ increases most rapidly. Since $-$grad $G(x)$ is the direction in which $G(x)$ decreases most rapidly, it is a promising direction in which to try to reduce $G(x)$ substantially.

In terms of everyday experience, one attempts to descend the surface $G(x)$ as fast as possible in order to arrive at the bottom. In principle the method will be successful so long as one can stay out of local minima of $G(x)$ which do not have the value zero. In practice, the descent is often prohibitively slow, even when nonzero minima do not intervene. The difficulty can be described for $n = 2$ by saying that one is stuck in the fog somewhere on the almost flat floor of a very narrow valley between two steep walls and is trying to reach the lowest point in the valley. Wherever one wanders, one continually runs into the walls without making much progress toward the lowest point. The possible difficulties are almost infinitely worse for values of n substantially greater than two. Thus, the choice of acceleration method is important in these problems.

Sometimes the nature of $G(x)$ is such that computing grad $G(x)$ is very difficult. Then one can often approximate the derivatives by finite-difference expressions. For example, one can approximate $\partial G(x)/\partial x_i$ at x^0 by the expression

$$[G(x^0 + he_i) - G(x^0 - he_i)]/2h,$$

where e_i is the i-th unit vector. Then the n difference expressions can be used together to approximate the gradient vector grad $G(x)$. Thus $2n$ evaluations of $G(x)$ can furnish a reasonable approximation of the gradient.

If the evaluation of $G(x)$ is expensive, it might pay to evaluate it only at the $n + 1$ vertices of a regular simplex in n space and then to approximate the derivatives by appropriate linear combinations of these $n + 1$ values. Such methods have been relatively little explored.

Problems where the evaluation of $G(x)$ is very expensive and evaluation of its gradient almost impossible occur, for example, where the evaluation of $G(x)$ requires the computation of a long trajectory.

In brief, descent methods for solving nonlinear systems can be used even where evaluation of derivatives is impractical.

In Newton methods, one makes a first guess x^0 and then approximates the nonlinear problem by a suitable linear problem involving derivatives of f_i evaluated at x^0. This linearized problem is a system of linear algebraic equations. Its solution furnishes an increment which is added to x^0 to give x^1, which is usually a better approximation to the solution of the nonlinear system. This process is iterated to convergence. The method is the precise generalization to n dimensions of Newton's process for finding zeros of a real function of a real variable.

In more detail, Newton's process is this: We are given a first guess x^0. We approximate each function f_i of (25.1) by two terms of its Taylor series at x^0:

$$(25.4) \qquad f_i(x) \doteq f_i(x^0) + \sum_{j=1}^{n} \frac{\partial f_i(x^0)}{\partial x_j} (x_j - x_j^0) \quad (i = 1, \ldots, n).$$

Let us denote by $J(x)$ the value at x of the Jacobian matrix of the system $f_i(x)$, i.e.,

$$J(x) = \begin{bmatrix} \dfrac{\partial f_1}{\partial x_1} & \cdots & \dfrac{\partial f_1}{\partial x_n} \\ \cdot & & \cdot \\ \cdot & & \cdot \\ \cdot & & \cdot \\ \dfrac{\partial f_n}{\partial x_1} & \cdots & \dfrac{\partial f_n}{\partial x_n} \end{bmatrix}$$

Then (25.4) takes the form

$$(25.5) \qquad\qquad f(x) \doteq f(x^0) + J(x^0)(x - x^0).$$

The right-hand side is the linear vector function of x which best approximates the nonlinear function f at the point x^0. It is the tangent hyperplane to the surface $f(x)$ at x^0. In Newton's process we set the right-hand side of (25.5) equal to θ and solve for x, giving the solution the name x^1. Thus

$$(25.6) \qquad\qquad x^1 := x^0 - [J(x^0)]^{-1} f(x^0).$$

Similarly, the general step of the iteration is

$$(25.7) \qquad\qquad x^{k+1} := x^k - [J(x^k)]^{-1} f(x^k).$$

In two dimensions the system (25.1) involves finding a point of intersection of two curves in the (x_1, x_2) plane—for example, $f(x_1, x_2) = 0$ and $g(x_1, x_2) = 0$. Consider the surface S_1 with equation $x_3 = f(x_1, x_2)$, and another surface S_2 with equation $x_3 = g(x_1, x_2)$. Surfaces S_1 and S_2 intersect on a curve C. The solution of (25.1) may also be interpreted as the point P where C crosses the plane, $x_3 = 0$. In Newton's process we effectively construct a tangent plane Π_1 to S_1 at x^k, and a second tangent plane Π_2 to S_2 at the same point. Then Π_1 and Π_2 intersect on a line L, which crosses the plane $x_3 = 0$ at the point x^{k+1}. Thus Newton's process replaces surfaces by tangent planes—this is the meaning of linearization in this case.

The calculation at each stage of the iteration involves evaluation of n^2 derivatives and the solution of a linear algebraic system to obtain the solution of (25.7). As with all equation solving, the evaluation of the residual vector $f(x^k)$ is the step which must be done with high precision. The Jacobian matrix itself need not be known very accurately; in fact one can often leave $J(x)$ unchanged throughout several steps of an iteration. As the reader will recall, this means a great economy in linear equation solving since the routine *SOLVE* can be used instead of the full linear-system package.

We have not discussed how to obtain a first guess x^0, and there is no ready answer. Often the originator of a problem knows enough about it to suggest a first guess which is close enough. At other times, one may have to use descent methods to get a first guess x^0. Sometimes, as in a parameter study, there are many problems, each differing only slightly from a previous one. Then the solution of one problem can often furnish the start for the next one.

The nature of the convergence of Newton's process is discussed in considerable detail in Henrici (1964). The following is known: Let a be a solution of the system (25.1): $f(a) = 0$. Assume that the functions f_i have several continuous derivatives. Then there is a certain number r such that $\|x^0 - a\| \leq r$ implies $x^k \to a$ as $k \to \infty$. Moreover, if $J(a)$ is nonsingular, then the convergence of x^k to a is quadratic or faster. That is,

$$\lim_{k \to \infty} \frac{\|x^{k+1} - a\|}{\|x^k - a\|^2}$$

exists as a finite nonnegative number (usually not zero). Quadratic convergence is ultimately very fast, in the sense that the number of good decimal digits eventually roughly doubles at each iterative step (until the round-off level is reached).

What happens if x^0 is far from any solution a? This is a complicated question, and the answer depends on f. Computing experience is that x^k will often eventually approach some solution a, but that it may jump around the space for quite a distance and for quite a number of steps. It may be impossible to guess which solution will be approached.

Finally, there will often be cases in which x^k does not converge. Instead, a small cycle of x^k may approach a number of limit points. This may occur, for example, if Newton's process for one variable is used with a real start x^0 when f has only complex zeros.

Despite the possible difficulties, it frequently pays to be optimistic. In the absence of knowledge of where the solutions a are or of how many there are, one picks some x^0 and starts the Newton algorithm. It often converges to something. One then starts somewhere else and finds another solution. In this way, one can often find a number of solutions of a nonlinear system. If it is required to find *all* the solutions, however, the above approach furnishes no clue as to when all have been found. Moreover, for some systems we frequently keep finding the same solution. The latter can often be prevented by changing the function, as follows: Suppose we have found a solution a of the system $f(x) = 0$. Now let

$$g(x) = f(x)/\|x - a\|.$$

If we apply Newton's process to the new function g, the zero of the numerator will presumably be balanced by the zero of the denominator, and this will keep iterates away from a. The evaluation of $g(x)$ is hardly more difficult for a given x than the evaluation of $f(x)$. However, the derivatives become more complicated, especially after several roots have been found and placed in analogous factors in the denominator.

Relatively little is reported about the solution of nonlinear systems. Now that we have such a reliable linear equation solver as a tool, it is possible to undertake research on nonlinear systems. The reader should consult Chap. 4 of Wendroff (1966) or Chapter 8 of Ralston (1965).

APPENDIX

(1). **Sketch of a proof of (8.21).** First prove that $a^2 + b^2 + c^2 + d^2$ and $|ad - bc|$ are invariant under the transformation from A to $U^T A V$ for any orthogonal matrices U, V. Then use (3.1) to transform A into

$$\begin{bmatrix} \mu_1 & 0 \\ 0 & \mu_2 \end{bmatrix}, \quad \text{where } \mu_1 \geq \mu_2 > 0.$$

Then
$$\sigma = \frac{\mu_1^2 + \mu_2^2}{2\mu_1\mu_2} = \frac{1}{2}\left(\frac{\mu_1}{\mu_2} + \frac{\mu_2}{\mu_1}\right)$$

$$= \tfrac{1}{2}[\text{cond }(A) + \text{cond }(A)^{-1}].$$

Solving the last equation for cond (A), we get

$$\text{cond }(A) = \sigma + \sqrt{\sigma^2 - 1},$$

since cond $(A) \geq 1$.

(2). **Partial solution of (6.5).** If A were singular, there would exist a vector $x = (x_1, \ldots, x_n)^T$ so that $Ax = 0$. Let $|x_k| = \max_j |x_j|$. Then

$$-a_{k,k}x_k = \sum_{\substack{j=1 \\ (j \neq k)}}^{n} a_{k,j}x_j.$$

Hence
$$|a_{k,k}| \leq \sum_{j \neq k} |a_{k,j}| \frac{|x_j|}{|x_k|}.$$

(a) Suppose there is a j such that $|x_k| > |x_j|$ and $|a_{k,j}| \neq 0$. Then

$$|a_{k,k}| < \sum_{j \neq k} |a_{k,j}|,$$

contradicting (6.2).

(b) We leave to the reader the case where (a) is not satisfied. See Taussky (1949) for a complete discussion.

BIBLIOGRAPHY AND AUTHOR INDEX

The following list includes all titles referred to in the text. Numbers in italics following a reference are pages of this book where the reference is cited. Names of authors referred to personally apart from a publication also appear in this list. Names associated only with a subject will be found in the Subject Index.

AMERICAN STANDARDS ASSOCIATION (1964), "A Programming Language for Information Processing on Automatic Data Processing Systems; FORTRAN vs. Basic FORTRAN," *Comm. Assoc. Comput. Mach.*, vol. 7, 591–625. *68*

ANONYMOUS (1960), *Information Processing; Proceedings of the International Conference on Information Processing, Unesco Paris 15–20 June 1959.* Paris: Unesco; Munich: R. Oldenbourg; and London: Butterworth & Co., Ltd., 520 pp. *138*

BAUER, F. L. (1960), "On the Definition of Condition Numbers and on Their Relation to Closed Methods for Solving Linear Systems," pp. 109–10 of Anonymous (1960). *24*

—— (1962), "Optimal Scaling of Matrices and the Importance of Minimal Condition," pp. 198–201 of C. M. Popplewell (1962).

—— (1963), "Optimally Scaled Matrices," *Numer. Math.*, vol. 5, 73–87. *38, 42, 43*

—— (see also R. Baumann).

BAUMANN, R., M. FELICIANO, F. L. BAUER, and K. SAMELSON (1964), *Introduction to Algol.* Englewood Cliffs, N.J.: Prentice-Hall, Inc., 142 pp. *58*

BENSTER, C. D. (see V. N. Faddeeva).

BOWDLER, H. J., R. S. MARTIN, G. PETERS, and J. H. WILKINSON (1966), "Solution of Real and Complex Systems of Equations," *Numer. Math.*, vol. 8, 217–34. *67*

BURROUGHS (1964), *B5500 Information Processing System Extended Algol Reference Manual.* Detroit, Mich.: Burroughs Corp., 100 pp. *72*

BUSINGER, PETER and GENE H. GOLUB (1965), "Linear Least Squares Solutions by Householder Transformations," *Numer. Math.*, vol. 7, 269–76. *17, 57*

CONTROL DATA (1963), *FORTRAN-63 Reference Manual*, Vols. I and II, Publication Numbers 527, 528. Palo Alto, Calif.: Control Data Corp. *68*

DANTZIG, GEORGE B. (1963), *Linear Programming and Extensions.* Princeton, N.J.: Princeton University Press, 627 pp. *13, 14*

FADDEEV, D. K. and V. N. FADDEEVA (1963), *Computational Methods of Linear Algebra* (translated by Robert C. Williams from a Russian book of 1960). San Francisco: W. H. Freeman and Co., 620 pp. *114*

FADDEEVA, V. N. (1959), *Computational Methods of Linear Algebra* (translated by C. D. Benster from a Russian book of 1950). New York: Dover Publications, Inc., 252 pp. *1, 2, 4*

——— (see also D. K. Faddeev).

FELICIANO, M. (see R. Baumann).

FORSYTHE, GEORGE E. (1958), "Singularity and Near Singularity in Numerical Analysis," *Amer. Math. Monthly*, vol. **65**, 229–40. *57*

——— (1960), "Algorithm 16; Crout with Pivoting in ALGOL 60," *Comm. Assoc. Comput. Mach.*, vol. **3**, 507–8. *58*

——— (1967), "Today's Computational Methods of Linear Algebra," *SIAM Review*, vol. **9**, to appear.

FORSYTHE, GEORGE E. and WOLFGANG R. WASOW (1960), *Finite Difference Methods for Partial Differential Equations*. New York: John Wiley & Sons, Inc., 444 pp. *120, 129–131*

FOX, L. (1964), *Introduction to Numerical Linear Algebra*. Oxford: Clarendon Press, 328 pp. *98*

GAUSS, C. F. *27*

GIVENS, WALLACE (1954), *Numerical Computation of the Characteristic Values of a Real Symmetric Matrix*, Report ORNL 1574. Oak Ridge, Tenn.: Oak Ridge National Laboratory, 107 pp. *95*

GOLUB, G. (1965), "Numerical Methods for Solving Linear Least Squares Problems," *Numer. Math.*, vol. **7**, 206–16. *17, 57*

——— (see also Peter Businger).

GOLUB, G. and W. KAHAN (1965), "Calculating the Singular Values and Pseudo-inverse of a Matrix," *J. SIAM Numer. Anal. Ser. B*, vol. **2**, 205–24. *17, 57*

HAMMING, R. W. *45n*

HENRICI, PETER (1964), *Elements of Numerical Analysis*. New York: John Wiley & Sons, Inc., 328 pp. *135*

HILBERT, D. (1894), "Ein Beitrag zur Theorie des Legendre'schen Polynoms," *Acta Math.*, vol. **18**, 155–60. *80*

HOUSEHOLDER, ALSTON S. (1953), *Principles of Numerical Analysis*. New York: McGraw-Hill Book Company, 274 pp. *95*

INTERNATIONAL BUSINESS MACHINES (1965a), *IBM 7090/7094 IBSYS Operating System; Version 13; FORTRAN IV Language*, IBM Systems Reference Library, File No. 7090-25, Form C28-6390-2. White Plains, N.Y.: IBM. *68*

——— (1965b), *IBM System/360: Basic Programming Support FORTRAN IV*, IBM Systems Reference Library, File No.S360-25, Form C28-6504-2. White Plains, N.Y.: IBM. *68*

———— (1966), *IBM Operating System/360; PL/I: Language Specifications*, IBM Systems Reference Library, File No. S360-29, Form C28-6571-2. White Plains, N.Y.: IBM. *74*

KAHAN, W. (1965a), "The Floating Point Over/Underflow Trap Routine FPTRP," *Programmers' Reference Manual*, Section 4.1. Toronto, Canada: University of Toronto, Institute of Computer Science, March 1965. *55*

———— (1965b), Writeups of library tape subroutines LEQU, LEQUN, FLEQU, CLEQU, DLEQU, to run under Toronto modifications of FORTRAN IV and MAP under IBSYS on a 7094-II. Toronto, Canada: University of Toronto, Institute of Computer Science, various months, 1965. *72*

———— (see also G. Golub). *97*

KLYUYEV, V. V. and N. I. KOKOVKIN-SHCHERBAK (1965), *On the Minimization of the Number of Arithmetic Operations for the Solution of Linear Algebraic Systems of Equations* (translated by G. J. Tee), Computer Science Department, Technical Report CS24. Stanford, Calif.: Stanford University. 24 pp. *32*

KOKOVKIN-SHCHERBAK, N. I. (see V. V. Klyuyev).

LANCZOS, CORNELIUS (1956), *Applied Analysis.* Englewood Cliffs, N.J.: Prentice-Hall, Inc., 539 pp. *95*

LUKACS, EUGENE (see I. Richard Savage).

MARTIN, R. S. (see H. J. Bowdler).

MARTIN, R. S., G. PETERS, and J. H. WILKINSON (1966), "Iterative Refinement of the Solution of a Positive Definite System of Equations," *Numer. Math.*, vol. **8**, 203–16. *61*

McKEEMAN, WILLIAM MARSHALL (1962), "Algorithm 135; Crout with Equilibration and Iteration," *Comm. Assoc. Comput. Mach.*, vol. **5**, 553–55. *45, 58*

MOLER, CLEVE B. (1964), "SOLVE, Accurate Simultaneous Linear Equation Solver with Iterative Improvement," SHARE distribution no. 3194.

———— (1967), "Iterative Refinement in Floating Point," *J. Assoc. Comput. Mach.*, vol. **14**, to appear. *109*

NATIONAL PHYSICAL LABORATORY (1961), *Modern Computing Methods*, 2nd ed., Notes on Applied Science No. 16. London: Her Majesty's Stationery Office, 170 pp.

NAUR, PETER (editor) *et al.* (1963), "Revised Report on the Algorithmic Language ALGOL 60," *Comm. Assoc. Comput. Mach.*, vol. **6**, 1–17. *58*

PETERS, G. (see H. J. Bowdler and R. S. Martin).

POPPLEWELL, C. M. (editor) (1962), *Information Processing.* Amsterdam: North-Holland Publishing Co., 780 pp. *138*

RALSTON, ANTHONY (1965), *A First Course in Numerical Analysis.* New York: McGraw-Hill Book Company, 578 pp. *67, 136*

SAMELSON, K. (see R. Baumann).

SAVAGE, I. RICHARD and EUGENE LUKACS (1954), "Table of Inverses of Finite Segments of the Hilbert Matrix," pp. 105–8 of Taussky (1954). *84*

TAUSSKY, OLGA (1949), "A Recurring Theorem on Determinants," *Amer. Math. Monthly*, vol. **51**, 672–76. *137*

—— (editor) (1954), *Contributions to the Solution of Systems of Linear Equations and the Determination of Eigenvalues*, U.S. National Bureau of Standards, Applied Mathematics Series, vol. **39**. Washington, D.C.: Supt. of Documents, 139 pp. *140*

TEE, G. J. (see V. V. Klyuyev).

TODD, JOHN (1954), "The Condition of the Finite Segments of the Hilbert Matrix," pp. 109–16 of Taussky (1954). *84*

—— (1961), "Computational Problems Concerning the Hilbert Matrix," *J. Research Nat. Bur. Standards, Ser. B.*, vol. **65**, 19–22. *84*

TORNHEIM, L. (1965), "Maximum Third Pivot for Gaussian Reduction," unpublished manuscript. Richmond, Calif.: California Research Corp., 10 pp. *108*

VARAH, JAMES *44*

VARGA, RICHARD S. (1962), *Matrix Iterative Analysis*. Englewood Cliffs, N.J.: Prentice-Hall, Inc., 322 pp. *14, 43, 130*

WASOW, WOLFGANG R. (see George E. Forsythe).

WENDROFF, BURTON (1966), *Theoretical Numerical Analysis*. New York: Academic Press, Inc., 239 pp. *36, 98, 117, 136*

WILKINSON, J. H. (1961), "Error Analysis of Direct Methods of Matrix Inversion," *J. Assoc. Comput. Mach.*, vol. **8**, 281–330. *35, 44–47, 98, 102*

—— (1963), *Rounding Errors in Algebraic Processes*. Englewood Cliffs, N.J.: Prentice-Hall, Inc., 161 pp. *87, 94, 98; 102, 107*

—— (1965), *The Algebraic Eigenvalue Problem*. Oxford: Clarendon Press, 662 pp. *98*

—— (see also H. J. Bowdler and R. S. Martin).

WILLIAMS, ROBERT C. (see D. K. Faddeev).

SUBJECT INDEX

This index includes names associated with a subject; for example, *Schwarz inequality*. Names mentioned with publications or in personal references will be found in the Bibliography and Author Index, pp. 138–41.